Berlitz®
Milan
& the Italian Lakes

Text by Patricia Schultz
Updated and edited by Clare Peel
Series Editor: Tony Halliday

D0493930

Berlitz® POCKET GUIDE

Milan
& the Italian Lakes

Eleventh Edition 2004

PHOTOGRAPHY
Chris Coe 13, 90, 99, 100; Jerry Dennis 6, 8, 9, 10, 18, 20, 22, 24, 26, 27, 28, 29, 30, 32–3, 34, 37, 38, 41, 49, 52, 53, 55, 56, 58, 59, 61, 62, 64, 66, 68, 70, 76/77, 79, 88, 94, 97, 102; Annabel Elston 72, 73, 74; Ros Miller 16, 39, 43; Alessandra Santarelli 48, 84, 86; George Taylor 80, 82, 93, 104.
Cover: Index Stock/Powerstock

CONTACTING THE EDITORS
Every effort has been made to provide accurate information in this publication, but changes are inevitable. The publisher cannot be responsible for any resulting loss, inconvenience or injury. We would appreciate it if readers would call our attention to any errors or outdated information by contacting Berlitz Publishing, PO Box 7910, London SE1 1WE, England.
Fax: (44) 20 7403 0290;
e-mail: berlitz@apaguide.co.uk
www.berlitzpublishing.com

Shop or have a coffee in style at Milan's most elegant city-centre arcade, the Galleria Vittorio Emanuele II (page 32)

The Navigli (page 56), the city's canal district, is a great place for an evening out

Milan's castle, Castello Sforzesco (page 38), houses a museum and an art gallery

TOP TEN ATTRACTIONS

Milan's so-called 'Golden Quadrilateral' (page 45) is back-to-back big-name designers

At the heart of Milan is the Duomo (page 27), the third-largest church in Christendom

Escape the city vibe of Milan by taking a trip to the nearby lakes (page 69). Como, shown here, is the closest lake to Milan

Leonardo's fresco, *The Last Supper* (page 52), can be viewed in the Refectory adjacent to Santa Maria delle Grazie

Historic Bergamo (page 65) is within easy reach of Milan

The Brera is home to the Pinacoteca di Brera (page 42) art gallery

Pavia's charterhouse (page 59) is the region's second most impressive monument

CONTENTS

A ➤ in the text denotes a highly recommended sight

INTRODUCTION

Milan is located in the Po Valley in the northwest of Italy. As capital of the Lombardy region, it shares the valley with the university town of Pavia, hilltop Bergamo and industrial Brescia. It is just 50km (30 miles) south of Switzerland.

The Secret Capital

For its energy, style and economic power, Milan should be the capital of Italy. In terms of contemporary Italian creativity, this is the place to be. In industry, fashion, and commerce, the city sets both tastes and standards for the whole country – and for much of Europe as well. There is a certain unique spirit in this city. Although Napoleon conquered many great cities in Europe, only Milan thought of erecting a statue of him in the nude, right in front of the Brera Museum. Among 19th-century edifices, the Galleria Vittorio Emanuele II is not just another shopping arcade, but an eloquent tribute to the industrial age of steel and glass. Then there is La Scala opera house: unprepossessing as it may look from the outside, in terms of its sublime interior and international prestige it has vast significance. And, of course, there is the city's monumental cathedral, the Duomo, completed over centuries.

Moving forward, the city's 1920s' railway station, the monumental and imposing Stazione Centrale, is an apt expression of Mussolini's questionable version of the modern age. The graceful Pirelli skyscraper, directly opposite, makes an aesthetically striking contrast.

> The Italians dub Milan their 'secret capital', *la capitale morale*. It is the second-largest city in the country, and Italy's main industrial and financial metropolis.

View from the top of the Duomo

And if all this modernity gets to be too much, you can always wander away from it with a stroll along the 16th-century canals *(navigli)* by the Porta Ticinese gate or head for the Parco Sempione, the gardens behind the Castello Sforzesco.

Living in Style

Milan's strategic location as a gateway between northern Europe and Italy has attracted many invaders over the centuries, notably the Spanish, French and Austrians. It was the Austrians of the 19th-century Hapsburg Empire, however, who left the most visible mark. There is more than a distinctive touch of Vienna in the sweep of ring roads around the old city centre *(centro storico)* and broad avenues lined with imposing Neo-Classical buildings.

Style is an essential part of the Milan ethos, and nowhere is it more apparent than in the exclusive shops on and around Via Montenapoleone – the area incorporating vias Montenapoleone, Mazoni, Sant'Andrea and della Spiga is known as Milan's *quadrilatero della moda*, or fashion quadrilateral. Here, couturiers from the great houses of Armani, Prada and Versace sit side by side with up-and-coming catwalk designers.

Milanese white taxi

The Milanese

The Milanese (few of whom are actually native to the city) are a hard-working bunch. Around one third of the city's population of 1.5 million is employed in industry, and the Milanese in general (3 percent of the national population) contribute one quarter of Italy's income-tax revenue.

Strolling through pretty Piazza Mercanti

Many people consider Milan to be the only truly cosmopolitan city in Italy – a genuine melting-pot with a large immigrant population. This hasn't always meant life has been easy, with clashes occurring between locals and immigrants both in the suburbs and the city centre. But history has shown that Milan has always understood how to learn from its immigrants, and there are hopes that these new citizens are gradually becoming better integrated.

There's an old expression, *El milanès el ga el cör in man*, which translates as 'the Milanese wears his heart on his sleeve'. The Italians generally see the Milanese as an honest, forthright bunch, refreshingly no-nonsense and reliable.

The Lakes
The attraction of Milan lies not just in the city itself – there is also the bonus of the surrounding countryside. Leave the city behind and escape to the tranquillity of the lakes, whose

waters lap the foothills of the Alps. Italy's famous trio of elongated lakes – Maggiore, Como and Garda – constitutes one of Europe's most romantic resort areas. Here you'll also find outstanding art museums in towns such as Bergamo, south of Milan, and the Carthusian monastery of Certosa di Pavia, a jewel of late Gothic and Renaissance art.

Many like to visit the lakes in spring, when there is a profusion of blossom, and the villas with their parks and gardens are utterly magnificent. Swimmers tend to favour early summer through to September as a good time for a holiday – the water is a very pleasant 25°C (77°F) in July and August. That said, autumn is ideal for long hikes and serene contemplation of (relatively) tourist-free scenery, and the service tends to be a lot better in the local restaurants because the staff are less pressed for time. Only in winter is it quiet, as many places close down for the season.

Enjoying the sun on Varenna's waterfront

A BRIEF HISTORY

Milan's first settlement was founded in 600BC as the capital of the Insubres, a Celtic tribe from Gaul. It was known as *Mediolanum*, 'town at the centre' – legend also goes that it was named after a half-woolly beast, its ancient founder according to a colourful folkloric tale of the city's origin.

After conquest by the Romans in 222BC, Milan became the major city of Cisalpine Gaul (Rome's Gallic lands south of the Alps). Under Emperor Augustus, it was second only to Rome itself. When the empire was split in two by Diocletian in the 3rd century, Milan was declared the western emperor's residential and administrative capital, and rapidly proved a lucrative trading centre between Italy and northern Europe.

Ambrose, Attila and the Lombards

It was a provincial governor, Aurelius Ambrosius, sent from Rome's German colony of Trier in AD 374, who placed Milan firmly on the European map. His reputation for justice and personal incorruptibility sparked such popular approval that he became bishop of Milan, and was later canonised. Thanks to St Ambrose's scrupulous leadership and resistance to less than scrupulous emperors, Milan became a pillar of the Christian church. To this day Ambrosius is still regarded as loving protector of the city, and he is its patron saint *(see box, page 54)*.

Passing through the town in AD 452, however, Attila the Hun showed unsurprisingly little respect for Milan's spiritual values, leaving a characteristic combination of rape and pillage in his wake. The Goths followed suit in AD538, burning the city to the ground. Some 30 years later, the Milanese clergy and their flock were on the run again, seeking the protection of Greek-led Byzantine forces around Genoa against the latest wave of invaders, the Lombards. Originally from north Germany, the *Longobardi,* or Long Beards, launched their attack on Italy from the Danube valley. Passing quickly through deserted Milan, rough King Alboin established his court at Pavia, which he captured from the Byzantines in AD572 after a three-year siege. He was murdered soon after, for forcing his wife to drink wine from her dead father's skull.

To show the locals that they were not entirely barbarian, the Lombards set up courts of law, established an important school of jurisprudence at Pavia, and gradually abandoned their traditional system of vendetta. Their empire expanded across Italy as far as the Duchy of Benevento, south of Naples.

The Lombards' most important king was Liudprand (AD 712–744), who, acting in the best interests of a tactical alliance with native Roman Catholics against the outsider Byzantines, managed to persuade his fellow Lombards to give up the Arian heresy *(see box, page 54)* that they had brought with them from Germany. By the time Charlemagne, king of the Franks, had conquered Lombardy, occupying Milan in AD 774, the people of Lombard and Roman stock had integrated to form what could be called the Italians.

The Middle Ages

In the 9th and 10th centuries, Milan bounced back. Yet again, it was the church that boosted the city's self-confidence. Under energetic Archbishop Ansperto da Biassono, the city walls were rebuilt. Trade soared, and the town soon showed off its prosperity through religious architecture *(see box, left)*. In 1045, the city declared itself a commune with autonomous government, and was vying for supremacy with its Lombard rivals, Pavia, Cremona, Lodi and Como.

Two of the city's finest churches, Sant' Ambrogio and Sant' Eustorgio, were built as a result of the trade boom in the Middle Ages.

Attracted by this new power and wealth, Frederick Barbarossa ('Redbeard') looked to annex Milan in his Holy Roman Empire. He smashed its city walls in 1162, but the Milanese forces resisted and the war continued until 1183. In the meantime, a new Lombard League was formed (1167) under Milan's leadership to repel the foreign invader.

On 29 May 1176, the Lombard League's troops, bearing the ferocious name of *Compagnia della Morte* (Company of Death), defeated Barbarossa's German forces at Legnano, northwest of Milan. The victory was

Milan is rich with glorious churches

vital for the national consciousness since for the first time the battle cry was heard for 'the freedom and honour of Italy'.

Rise and Fall of the Visconti

The 13th century ushered in the era of the great dynastic families. The Ghibelline forces of Archbishop Ottone Visconti (supporting the emperor) routed the Torriani family representing the Guelph faction (supporting the pope) at Desio in 1277. With a family name derived from a hereditary 11th-century title of viscount, the Archbishop Visconti was succeeded in 1295 by his great-nephew Matteo Visconti, who imposed an authoritarian rule over the commune and region. In gratitude for his military support, the German King Adolf of Nassau bestowed on him the title of Imperial Vicar of Lombardy. When this aroused the ire of Pope John XXII, Matteo (1250–1322) settled for *Signore* (Lord) of Milan. However, he did not escape excommunication on charges of heresy.

Milan prospered under the *signoria* (lordship). Its urban population of over 200,000 was Europe's largest. Trade and industry (mainly textiles and metalwork) boomed, and Matteo controlled Milan and much of Lombardy with an army of mercenaries; there were no communal forces to resist, and the merchants were too busy making money to care much about military matters. Enriched by lands outside Milan and ensured of the support of the German emperor, the Visconti had broken free of dependence on the hitherto demanding local populace.

The Visconti were also great patrons of the arts, starting work on the Duomo, founding the Certosa di Pavia, and making the University of Pavia one of the finest in Europe. Gian Galeazzo Visconti (1351–1402) was a disciple of the poet Petrarch, whom he made director of the Visconti library. He also developed a modern bureaucracy, conceiving state and government as a rationally planned 'work of art.' In 1395 he bought the title of Duke of Milan, and through an alliance with Isabelle de Valois married into the French royal family. Their daughter, Valentina, married the French king's brother.

Gian Galeazzo's hold on power led him to ignore his nominal allegiance to the German emperor. He hired and fired at will, imposed taxes and laws without consulting the duchy's council, enforced mail-censorship, and controlled travel by introducing passports. The lands he expropriated at strategic points gave him almost total control of northern Italy, culminating in his seizure of Bologna in 1402. That same year, with his lordship established over Pisa, Siena and Perugia, he was poised to attack Florence when the plague carried him off.

Visconti court etiquette had become highly refined and elaborate, distancing the rulers from the people. Arbitrary tax-gouging and law enforcement characterised an authority dependent entirely on autocratic rule. Thus, under Gian Galeazzo's mad heir, Giovanni Maria, the Visconti Empire quickly fell apart. By 1447 the dynasty had died out, though the female line passed through the Visconti to the Valois of France (notably Louis XII and François I, who were to stake claims to the duchy of Milan), as well as the Hapsburgs of Austria and Spain, and the Tudors of England.

Renaissance under the Sforzas

The day after the death of the last Visconti despot, Filippo Maria, Milan established an 'Ambrosian Republic'. Born from an unresolved power struggle between rival factions of aristocrats rather than a popular movement for democracy, it proved unable to control its hinterland and lasted only three years before yielding to Francesco Sforza in 1450. The *condottiere* (captain) asserted his claim to the duchy as the husband of an illegitimate Visconti daughter, Bianca Maria.

The powerful Sforza family had left their farms in Romagna, near Ravenna, to become mercenaries, offering their services in rapid succession to Ferrara, Naples and Milan. When Francesco fell out with the Visconti family, he joined

Bianca Maria Sforza

Drawing by Milan's most famous son, Leonardo da Vinci

the Medici of Florence and fought for them against Milan. Once installed as Duke of Milan, he actually formed an alliance with the Florentines against Venice and Naples.

Although no less despotic than the Visconti, the Sforza dynasty restored prosperity, particularly through expansion of the arms and silk industries, and brought a new artistic luster to the city. With his son, Galeazzo Maria Sforza, Francesco built the splendid Ospedale Maggiore and restored the formidable Castello Sforzesco. His other son, Ludovico, completed the bulk of the work on the cathedral and built a great tribune for the Church of Santa Maria delle Grazie and cloister for the Church of Sant' Ambrogio. He also expanded the network of canals for trade, and strengthened the city fortifications for defence against his enemies.

Deriving his nickname from his dark complexion and black hair, Ludovico il Moro ('the Moor') was politically less astute than his father but culturally the most brilliant of the Sforza dukes. He was a typical Renaissance prince, ruthless in government, devious in diplomacy, and enlightened in his patronage of the arts. Among his protégés were the great architect Donato Bramante and Leonardo da Vinci. His court's glittering life was famous across Europe.

Ludovico's lust for power pitted him against his mother in wresting the duchy from its rightful heir, his seven-year-old nephew, Gian Galeazzo, who had been 'exiled' to a rival court in Pavia. Ludovico made and broke alliances with bewildering facility first with Naples against Venice, then with France against Naples, and finally with Venice against France. He remained, however, relatively loyal to his father-in-law, the Duke of Ferrara, and to the German emperor, Maximilian I, who had formally confirmed his right to the title of duke.

His machinations did get the better of him when, fearing trouble from Gian Galeazzo's followers, he encouraged the invasion by Charles VIII of France to seize the throne of Naples in 1494. This fatal blunder marked the beginning of the end – not only for the duchy itself, but also for all of Italy's independent city states.

Alarmed by the success of Charles VIII's military campaign, Ludovico then backed a Venice-led league to drive the French back out of Italy the following year. He emerged

Leonardo da Vinci

As Renaissance men went, few could match the talents of Tuscany-born Leonardo da Vinci (1452–1519), whose skills covered everything from mathematics and botany to aviation, sculpture, architecture and, of course, painting. In 1482, when he left Florence for the court of Ludovico Sforza in Milan, his calling card was that of a musician. In his application for work, Leonardo himself listed his talents as a builder of cannons and fortifications, and master of piping for water and heat. He added as an afterthought: 'I can carry out sculpture in marble, bronze or clay, and...in painting I can do as well as any man.' In his 18 prolific years in Milan, Leonardo spent most of his time as a glorified odd-job man around the Castello Sforzesco. In spare moments, he painted *The Last Supper* (1495–97) at Santa Maria delle Grazie *(see page 52)*, *Portrait of a Musician* at the Ambrosiana, the *Virgin of the Rocks*, now in the Louvre, and the *Litta Madonna*, now in the Hermitage in St Petersburg.

from the campaign as a short-term winner, boasting that Pope Alexander VI was now his chaplain, Emperor Maximilian his general, the Doge of Venice his chamberlain, and King Charles VIII his courier, but he had set in motion events that would prove his downfall. The historical novel *Duchess of Milan* details this period quite well; although a work of fiction, it includes actual excerpts from Leonardo da Vinci's correspondence.

In 1499, King Louis XII, grandson on his mother's side of Valentina Visconti, declared the Sforzas to be usurpers and marched into Milan to claim the duchy for himself. Tired of paying heavy taxes to support the luxury of the Sforza court and the cost of the wars, the Milanese cheered their new master. Ludovico attempted a comeback in 1500, but was roundly defeated and spent the rest of his life in exile, in the gilded prison of a Loire Valley château.

Resurrection fresco, Castello Sforzesco

Foreign Rule

For the next 360 years, Milan was a pawn in the rivalries of Spain, France and Austria. Among the few highlights in two centuries of gloom were the educational reforms of the city's archbishop, Carlo Borromeo (1538–84).

> Conditions in the dark era of Milan's history are strikingly depicted in the celebrated novel of Alessandro Manzoni, *The Betrothed*, an essential read for all Italian school children.

In 1706, during the War of Spanish Succession, the Hapsburgs installed Prince Eugene of Savoy as governor to enforce Austrian administration. The city was slow to emerge from stagnation, but in the second half of the 18th century the economy began to pick up. At this time, wealthy merchants built the first of the neoclassical buildings that dominate Milan today. Cultural oppression, however, particularly in the form of censorship, drove writers and sociologists to form the *Società dei Pugni* (literally, Society of Fists), espousing the ideas of the French Revolution.

After France's convincing defeat of the Austrians, Napoleon Bonaparte's soldiers were welcomed into the city as liberators in 1796. The Cisalpine Republic was proclaimed and the town flourished. In 1805, a grateful merchant bourgeoisie applauded the republic's transformation into the Kingdom of Italy, with Milan as capital, and Napoleon crowned himself king in the cathedral. Despite France's controlling involvement, Milan became the dominant force in Italian trade. It developed a proud new image, modernised by Napoleonic reforms in administration, scientific academies, and French-style secondary education for both boys and girls.

However, progress was halted by the collapse of the Napoleonic Empire and the return of conquering Austrian forces in 1814. Milan remained under Hapsburg rule for another 50 years. Though eager to exploit the city's prosperity, the regime remained as oppressive as ever. This time, imbued with a new self-assurance from contact with the French, the Milanese were quick to resist. Poised at the forefront of the *Risorgimento* movement for national unity, the Milanese staged an important revolt in March 1848. They liberated the city for a glorious but brief four months before being brutally crushed by the Austrian army. Several streets and squares all over Lombardy are named after those significant five days, *Cinque Giornate*.

Following victory over the Austrians at Marengo in 1859, Vittorio Emanuele, the first king of independent Italy, entered the city with his French ally Napoleon III. They came in through the triumphal arch (now known as Arco della Pace), which had been designed for the French emperor's uncle 50 years earlier.

Monument to Vittorio Emanuele II, Piazza del Duomo

Thereafter, Milan remained in the vanguard of Italy's belated but dynamic industrial and commercial revolution. In the boom years, metal, chemical and textile factories sprang up around the city's periphery, while publishing companies, banks, and the stock exchange dominated the centre. In the bold iron-and-glass roof of the Galleria Vittorio Emanuele shopping arcade *(see page 32)*, progress was given an architectural symbol. Leaving the political tangle to Rome, Milan was content with its role as the country's business capital, a division of power and attitude that survives to this day.

Freedom and Fascism

At the turn of the 20th century, the city was a hotbed of radical political movement. It had elected its first Socialist mayor in the 1890s, and the Milanese newspapers, publishers and university had assembled Italy's most progressive minds. In 1898, with the conservatives back in power, food riots protesting high wheat prices (essential for the daily pasta) led to the closure of the university and the presence of the army to enforce control. Its cannons left 100 dead and 600 wounded, including monks fired on by mistake when a crowd of beggars was waiting for soup outside their monastery.

It was in Milan in 1919 that Benito Mussolini founded his *Fasci Italiani di Combattimento* or Italian Combat League, simply known to history as the Fascists. In a hall lent by a circle of local merchants and industrialists, the ex-Socialist newspaperman assembled 60 anti-parliamentarians stirred by the ultranationalist sentiments of World War I. They started their campaign by drowning out Democratic speeches held at La Scala, but quickly moved to more characteristic activities such as burning the Milan headquarters of the Socialist newspaper, *Avanti!* After fanning the flames of the Movement across the country, *il Duce* returned to Milan in 1922 to mastermind the march on Rome of 26,000 Blackshirts. So ended Italy's brief experience of democracy.

Fascism was an ambivalent, and ultimately horrific, experience for Milan. Archbishop Ildefonso Schuster and Monsignor Agostino Gemelli, rector of the Catholic University, proved enthusiastic supporters of the cause, but the town was also a principal centre for the anti-Fascist group *Giustizia e Libertà*.

In World War II, the city suffered 15 bombardments, the heaviest of which occurred in 1943. The following year, Milan staged the nation's first general strike in protest against the war, leading to hundreds of workers being deported to German concentration camps. Fascist militia hanged 15 partisans on the Piazza Loreto where, just nine months later, Fascist leaders themselves were executed by partisan firing squads, and the corpses of Mussolini and his mistress Clara Petacci were strung up just a stone's throw from the Stazione Centrale, Mussolini's own monument in Milan.

After 1945, Milan recovered quickly, taking a leading role in the country's economic miracle. It has long boasted to have the lion's share of Italy's major banks, its stock market and its trade fairs. And Milan's suburbs are home to a range of heavy industries. In 1993, the discredited Socialist party, which for years had made the mayoralty its domain, gave way to the right-wing party of the Lombard League. In 1994, this was repeated in national elections, when the League, with Milan's TV-mogul Silvio Berlusconi's *Forza Italia* and the far-right National Alliance Party *(Alleanza Nazionale)*, the former neo-Fascist MSI party, gained the victory. (Berlusconi, as Prime Minister, would go on to form Italy's 59th post-war government in June 2001.)

Financial affairs are big business in contemporary Milan

Constantly changing politics are harder to keep up with than the rise and fall of the catwalk's hemlines. Through it all, the Milanese continue to succeed at what they do best: hard work and hard play.

Historical Landmarks

600 BC	First settlement established by the Gauls.
222 BC	Conquest by the Romans.
3rd cent. BC	Mediolanum is capital of Western Roman Empire.
452	Attila the Hun plunders the city.
568	The Lombards invade and make Pavia their capital.
774	Charlemagne enters Milan, ending Lombard rule.
1045	Milan constitutes itself an autonomous commune.
1176	Lombard League defeats Barbarossa at Legnano.
1277	Ghibelline Visconti defeat Guelf Torriani at Desio. Milan is Europe's largest city (pop. 200,000).
1351–1402	Gian Galeazzo Visconti starts Milan's Cathedral.
1447–50	Ambrosian Republic.
1450–66	Francesco Sforza becomes Duke of Milan.
1466–99	Ludovico Sforza sponsors Leonardo da Vinci.
1499	King Louis XII of France seizes Duchy of Milan.
1535	Control seized by Charles V.
1540–1706	Spanish rule.
1706	Prince Eugene of Savoy installs Austrian regime.
1796–1814	Napoleon makes Milan capital of his Cisalpine Republic, then of the Kingdom of Italy (1805).
1814–59	Rise of *Risorgimento* independence movement.
1859	Milan heads Italy's industrial revolution.
1890s	First Socialist city government is elected.
1919	Mussolini founds the Fascist movement in Milan.
1939–1945	World War II; Milan suffers heavy bombardment.
1993	Right-wing Lombard League mayor elected.
1994	Berlusconi's *Forza Italia* wins general election.
1995	Maurizio Gucci murdered in Milan.
2001	La Scala Opera House closes for renovation.
2002	The euro replaces the lira as Italy's main unit of currency.
2003	Prime Minister Silvio Berlusconi appears in court in Milan on corruption charges; immunity laws bring the trial to a halt.

WHERE TO GO: MILAN

The region of Lombardy, covering Milan and the lakes, can be divided into five areas for sightseeing. The city of Milan itself; excursions to the nearby towns of Pavia, Monza and Bergamo (all possible day trips from Milan); and the lakes, which we feature in a separate section *(see pages 69–83)*.

Even though Milan is one of the largest Italian cities, you can get a good feel for its most interesting attractions in just a day or two, as many of its churches, monuments and museums are concentrated in and around the centre. Start in the central area around the Duomo (cathedral) and La Scala Opera House, taking time to visit the shopping district around Via Montenapoleone. Then head for the grand Castello Sforzesco and its park before going west, to see Leonardo's *The Last Supper,* his science museum, and the church of Sant'Ambrogio.

Most of Milan's major sights are within comfortable walking distance. The tram-and-bus system can be tricky to negotiate, but the well-organized subway (Metropolitana) is straightforward and self-explanatory.

Keep a few hours for the Brera Museum and the nearby galleries, and then take your pick from the other museums and churches in the city. Those with more time might choose to explore Milan's outskirts, and between sights you can relax on a café terrace, perhaps in the canal district (known as the Navigli); from here you can watch the parade of fashionable Milanese while you sip an *aperitivo* and contemplate the many aspects of Italy's most vibrant metropolis.

Statue in the shady cloisters of the Castello Sforzesco

Piazza del Duomo

PIAZZA DEL DUOMO AND VICINITY

Few of the world's great cities have such an obvious focus for beginning a visit as the **Piazza del Duomo**. Rounding the corner of the piazza, your breath is taken away by the sheer grandness and flamboyant detail of the cathedral commanding the square. Designed by Giuseppe Mengoni, architect of the adjoining Galleria Vittorio Emanuele II, the square and arcades around the cathedral have for centuries provided a natural meeting place for both the Milanese and their pigeons.

As both the geographical and psychological centre of Milan, there is nonstop bustle during the day. Have a seat on the steps in front of the Duomo and catch a glamorous model walking by, a smartly dressed banker on his lunch break, a student sketching or an Italian television diva waiting to meet her agent. As the sun sets, and the late-afternoon *passeggiata*, or stroll, gets under way, you will see the bars under the Portici Settentrionali filling up with stylishly dressed men and women having a drink and nibbling on bar snacks before their dinner appointments.

The Duomo

Milan's **Duomo** (Cathedral; open daily 6.45am–6.45pm; note that you will not be allowed in if you're wearing shorts, a mini skirt or if your shoulders are uncovered) is the most grandiose of Italy's Gothic cathedrals. Begun in 1386 on the site of an earlier church (Santa Maria Maggiore), it took nearly six centuries to complete. The exterior of the cathedral was completely restored in time for the 2000 Jubilee, and the colour of the cathedral's white marble – taken from the nearby lake district – is resplendent even on a typically grey Milan day.

Duke Gian Galeazzo Visconti founded the church as a votive offering to God in his plight for a male heir. His plan worked, but his architectural demands proved too much for the local masons from nearby Lake Como, and French, Flemish and German architects had to be called in to help. The major Italian contribution was by Pellegrino Tibaldi, who worked in the 16th century mainly on the interior, under the direction of revered Archbishop Carlo Borromeo. The main spire was erected in the 18th century, the façade was completed under Napoleon in 1813, and work on other spires and exterior sculpture continued right up until the 20th century.

To best take in the bristling silhouette of marble pinnacles and statues and the awesomely flamboyant façade, stand on the

Duomo main door detail

south side of the cathedral in the courtyard of the Palazzo Reale *(see page 29)*. Despite the quite visible northern European influence, the Duomo presents a much wider and more 'horizontal' appearance than the majority of Gothic cathedrals in France and Germany.

The Cathedral Interior

Inside, the vast and noble space of the nave and four aisles shows more clearly the church's northern inspiration, particularly in the 52 soaring columns and the decoration of **stained-glass windows**, dating from the 15th century to the present day. The most precious stained glass, tracing the

Stained glass in the Duomo

story of St John the Evangelist, is to be seen in the south aisle (to the right). A 13th-century Visconti archbishop lies in the red marble sarcophagus mounted on pillars. In the right-hand transept, notice the matter-of-fact treatment of an horrific martyrdom in Marco d'Agrate's 1562 **statue of St Bartholomew**: flayed alive, he is carrying his own skin.

A door to the right of the high altar leads down to the cathedral's **crypt**, where you can see an ancient reliquary and ivory carvings from the 4th and 5th centuries. The remains of Archbishop Carlo Borromeo are displayed here, draped in opulent finery.

Back in the north transept is the 14th-century **Trivulzio Candelabrum**, with its seven branches of bronze.

In the cathedral's west façade, a separate entrance leads to the octagonal, 4th-century **baptistery**, where St Ambrose baptised St Augustine in 387.

The *Madonnina*

Make some time for every traveller's favourite Milanese experience: a spectacular walk out on the **roof** (*le terraze*; open Mar–Oct 9am–5.45pm, Nov–Feb 9am–4.15pm) – in warmer weather, the profane can cultivate a suntan here. The terraces can be reached by taking a lift at the northeast side of the cathedral. The entrance is on the outside of the building. There are quite a few steps to climb at the top of the lift, so it's advisable to wear comfortable, flat shoes.

Wander high above the city, beneath the flying buttresses and around the statues (2,245 in all) and pinnacles (135), and climb up to the roof ridge for an unbeatable view of Milan – with the not-too-distant Alps on those rare days that pollution does not veil their proximity. The Duomo's highest pinnacle is crowned by the golden statue of the *Madonnina* to whom the city's anthem is dedicated.

Palazzo Reale

South of the cathedral (adjoining the main Tourist Office at the corner of Via Marconi), the **Palazzo Reale**, former residence of Milan's Spanish and Austrian governors, today houses the **Museo del Duomo** (Cathedral Museum; open daily 10am–1.15pm and 3–6pm) in its south wing. It displays cathedral artefacts from the 14th to 19th centuries, including impressive Gothic sculpture from the cathedral exterior, casts of the countless statues gracing the Duomo's rooftop, a likeness of Gian Galeazzo Visconti, handsome 15th-century stained glass, Tintoretto's *Child Jesus with the Rabbis,* and a model of the Duomo as it was conceived in 1519.

On the palazzo's upper floor (accessible from the main courtyard) is the **Civico Museo di Arte Contemporaneo** (better known as CIMAC, Museum of Modern Art; galleries open Tues–Sun 9.30am– 5.30pm), a superb summary of the works of European artists from the late 19th century to the present day. The collection consists partly of art that was obtained during the course of the 20th century and partly of

Palazzo Reale, seen here from the roof of the Duomo, was the residence of the Viscontis in the early 14th century

paintings donated by the collectors Ausonio Canavese (includings works by the Futurist Umberto Boccioni) and Antonio Boschi, as well as from the artists Lucio Fontana and Fausto Melotti. Strong emphasis is also given to the Futurists and abstract artists, with works by Gino Rossi, Amedeo Modigliani, Alberto Savinio, Giorgio de Chirico, Gino Severini and Giorgio Morandi.

CIMAC's contemporary art collection (work made since the 1990s) is now on show at the Museo del Presente (Officine del gas di Bovisa, Via Giampietrino 24; Metro: Bovisa), a huge converted gasworks. This major addition to the Milanese art scene will feature temporary shows and works designed for this space.

> Located almost directly south of the Duomo is Torre Velasca, a brutalist skyscraper designed by Studio BBPR, the Milanese architectural group of Banfi, Belgiojoso, Peressutti & Rogers, in the late 1950s. The firm's work combines strong influence of both the Bauhaus and traditional Italian architectural styles – the cantilevered upper section, for example, is strongly reminiscent of the design of a traditional Italian fortress.

San Gottardo al Palazzo

The Palazzo Reale complex also contains the former ducal chapel of **San Gottardo al Palazzo** (entrance in Via Pecorari; Mon–Fri 8am–noon and 2–6pm, Sat 8am–4pm, Sun 8am–1pm). It was built in 1336 by Francesco Pecorari and, like the Palazzo Reale, was redesigned in 1770 in the neoclassical style by Piermarini. The warm brick tones of the tower form a stunning contrast to the white of the columns at its top. The unusual apse, which has gable windows and a dwarf gallery (an arcaded wall-passage on the outside of the building), dates from the 14th century.

Galleria Vittorio Emanuele II

Back on the north side of the Piazza del Duomo, through a triumphal arch, is a massive, cross-shaped shopping arcade, **Galleria Vittorio Emanuele II**. This grand steel-and-glass vaulted edifice is a monument to the expansive commercial spirit of the 19th century.

For cafés such as the famous Zucca's, restaurants, boutiques, bookshops and travel agencies, architect Giuseppe Mengoni provided an appropriate Neo-Renaissance décor delightfully cool in summer, but a little drafty in winter.

Galleria Vittorio Emanuele II

Sadly, a couple of days before the gallery's inauguration in 1878, Mengoni plunged to his death from scaffolding on the roof. Sadder still, American fast-food chains have elbowed in between the beautiful antique traditional cafés, although there is still a branch of Milanese fashion label Prada here, plus a major branch of Rizzoli booksellers, and institutions such as café-restaurant Savini.

If you feel like you need a little luck, take a spin on the 'balls of the bull' depicted on the western part of the intricate central mosaic flooring. Tradition dictates that anyone who spins on their left heel 360 degrees in one go will have good luck for their duration of their stay in Milan.

La Scala

The Galleria offers a convenient passage from the Duomo to Piazza alla Scala and, on the northwest side of the square, another holy of holies, the **Teatro alla Scala** (closed for renovation until late 2004), or La Scala, as the world-renowned opera house is familiarly known.

Given the prestige of the house – to have an engagement here still remains the pinnacle of many performers' careers – the plain, neo-classical exterior of the building is rather disappointing. Inside, however, things are more impressive. With its 2,000 seats, La Scala is still by far the largest theatre in Europe; its large mirror-lined upstairs foyer and lush, deep-red and gold auditorium are staggeringly opulent, and the theatre's acoustics are exceptional. The opening of the opera season on the day of the city's patron saint, St Ambrose (7 December), is still the greatest society event of the year in Milan.

While the extensive renovation is being carried out, performances are being held at the **Teatro degli Arcimbaldi** (Viale dell'Innovazione; Metro: Precotto then special bus), designed by Vittorio Gregotti and located in the Bicocca district to the north of the city. Information on ticket availability is supplied by an electronic terminal next to the ticket office at the Duomo metro station *(see also page 89)*.

The existence of Milan's original opera house is principally thanks to Empress Maria Theresa. After the Teatro Regio Ducale burned down in 1776, Maria Theresa approved the plan for a new theatre, although only 'at the expense of the people of Milan' (in the end she generously

La Scala opera house and the square that takes its name

covered most of the costs herself). Constructed in understated neoclassical style by Giuseppe Piermarini, the building stands on the site of the old church of Santa Maria della Scala, which had been donated in 1385 by Regina della Scala, the wife of Bernabò Visconti – hence the name of today's opera house. The ceremonial opening took place on 3 August 1778 with a performance of *L'Europa Riconosciuta* (Europe's Recognition), an opera by the Vienna court composer Antonio Salieri; adversary of Mozart and teacher of Beethoven, Schubert and Liszt.

Numerous world-class composers have cut their teeth in Milan, including Rossini, Donizetti, Bellini and Verdi. The international success of Giacomo Puccini's tragic opera *Madame Butterfly* (his second version, the one we hear today) also started at La Scala. Two other classical music stars linked with La Scala include the composer Arturo Toscanini and soprano, Maria Callas *(see box below)*.

(Note that the Museo Teatrale, formerly housed at La Scala has now moved to Corso Magento, *see page 55*).

Back in Piazza La Scala, opposite the Opera House, is Milan's 16th-century town hall, **Palazzo Marino**. In the middle of the square is a restored yet unprepossessing 19th-century monument to Leonardo and his pupils.

Opera Diva

Inextricably linked with La Scala, and heavily documented at the Museo Teatrale *(see page 55)*, is Maria Callas (1923–77). Born in New York, to immigrant Greek parents, she opened the season at La Scala in 1951 to great acclaim. Over the next seven years the Milanese opera house provided a stage for her greatest triumphs. In May 1958, however, she quarrelled with the director, Antonio Ghiringhelli, and decided not to sing while the house was under his control. She never performed here again.

Piazza Mercanti

Return now to Piazza del Duomo. From the northwest corner of the Piazza del Duomo, take Via Mercanti, leading to the only medieval area in the city to have survived the bombs of World War II and the wrecking ball of zealous post-war building developers. Before the cathedral was built, Piazza Mercanti was the centre of city life, with the seat of communal government, the Romanesque **Palazzo della Ragione** (1233), on its south side. It was the birthplace of the Milanese 'stock market,' as all trade and bartering of goods was carried out under its porticoes. Notice the relief of a *scrofa semilanuta*, a wild boar-like animal that is claimed to be the city's namesake.

The Ambrosiana

To the west of Piazza del Duomo is Milan's financial area, *Milano finanziario*, with the city's stock exchange on Piazza Affari. Near here is one of Milan's most distinguished art collections, housed in the Palazzo dell'Ambrosiana. Allow at least a couple of hours to visit the museum.

Situated on Piazza Pio XI, 2, the Ambrosiana has recently undergone a full renovation. Its great library, the **Biblioteca Ambrosiana** (open Mon–Fri 9.30am–5pm), was originally housed in the 17th-century palace of the illustrious Cardinal Federigo Borromeo (nephew of the great Italian churchman, Archbishop Carlo Borromeo). Among its precious manuscripts are Leonardo da Vinci's drawings, which illustrate his scientific and artistic theories.

The Ambrosiana's superb art gallery, the **Pinacoteca di Ambrosiana** (open Tues–Sun 10am–5.30pm; last entry one hour prior to closing time), has as one of its most precious treasures Leonardo's luminous *Portrait of a Musician* (1485), unfinished but the best preserved of the master's few surviving works. You can see his pervasive influence on

Milanese artists in the decorative paintings of Bernardino Luini and in the *Portrait of a Young Woman* by artist Ambrogio de Predis.

There's nothing sweet about Caravaggio's *Bowl of Fruit* – the worm is already in the apple and the leaves are withering. Titian is also well represented at the Ambrosiana, notably with an imposing *Adoration of the Magi*.

One of the most fascinating exhibits in the Pinacoteca collection, however, is by Raphael, particularly for those who know his great *School of Athens* fresco in the Vatican; in the Ambro-

The Ambrosiana

siana are the great Renaissance master's so-called 'cartoons' – his preparatory drawings for the Vatican piece.

San Satiro

Just off the busy Via Torino near the Ambrosiana library *(see page 36)*, **San Satiro** is a major work of Renaissance modelling (1478) by Donato Bramante. Walk around to Via Falcone to view its fine exterior, the 11th-century campanile and newly restored **Cappella della Pietà**. The handsome interior has a characteristic Milanese décor of terracotta. A Greek cross space is created by an optical illusion. Over the high altar is a 13th-century *Madonna and Child* fresco. Notice the elegant, octagonal Renaissance **baptistery** off the south (right) aisle.

CASTLE DISTRICT

➤ To the northwest of Piazza del Duomo is **Castello Sforzesco** (grounds open daily 8am–8pm; museums open Tues–Sun 9.30am–5.30pm), a sprawling fortress built by the Viscontis in the 14th century and expanded by the Sforza dynasty from the mid-15th century. The castle is home to several museums, including an ancient arts museum, a gallery and one of Europe's best museums of musical instruments. It's certainly worth a visit, whether for a meander through the attractive grounds, or a more lengthy look at the collection. Behind the castle is one of Milan's two main green spaces, Parco Sempione.

Castello Sforzesco tower

Castello Sforzesco

This huge brick fortress northwest of the city centre (Metro: Cairoli) was rebuilt in its present form in the 15th century by Duke Francesco Sforza. It stands on the site of a Visconti castle destroyed by citizens of the short-lived Ambrosian Republic *(see page 15)*. Used by the Spanish as a stronghold and by the Austrians as a refuge from the Italian uprising of 1848, it was converted to an art museum in the 1950s.

The four-square structure surrounds an interior courtyard, **Piazza d'Armi**, where fine summer concerts are held among the architectural fragments assembled here from other city monuments.

The main tower follows a Renaissance design by Florentine architect Antonio Filarete, and is therefore named after him. Roman master Donato Bramante contributed part of the other work, with some interior décor – and plumbing *(see page 17)* – by Renaissance man Leonardo da Vinci.

The Sforza coat of arms

The palace apartments were in the **Corte Ducale** over to the right, now the entrance to the **Musei del Castello** (Castle Museums), which has a pioneering modern art display in an antique setting. Inside the Ducal Courtyard is an open-air hall and portico commissioned by Galeazzo Maria Sforza in the late 15th century. The portico is known as the Portico dell'Elefante after its elephant fresco by Benedetto Ferrini.

The *Arte Antica* collections of ancient and medieval art are devoted mostly to sculpture, notably including a Roman sarcophagus and some interesting statuary from Byzantine, Romanesque and Gothic churches. Notice, too, the Gothic tombs of Bernabò Visconti, one of the more sadistically violent members of the Visconti clan, and his wife Regina della Scala, whose name survives in the opera house *(see page 35)*.

The **frescoes** in room 8, *Sala delle Asse,* in the northeast corner of the castle were done by Leonardo da Vinci but have since been badly damaged by unfortunate over-restoration.

Room 15, *Sala degli Scarlioni,* is reserved for the Castello Sforzesco's unfinished – but still remarkable – treasure,

Michelangelo's *Rondanini Pietà*

Michelangelo's ***Rondanini Pietà***. Named after its original home in the Palazzo Rondanini in Rome, the sculpture is a poignant, vertical treatment of Mary struggling to hold up the body of her crucified son.

Michelangelo worked on the piece on and off for nine years and was still chiselling away at it just six days before his death in 1564. There is a strange pathos in the great Renaissance master returning to Gothic forms for his last work in his 89th year. Nearby is a bronze bust of Michelangelo by his sculptor friend, Daniele da Volterra.

On the other side of the Corte Ducale, the **Pinacoteca** is home to important paintings by masters including Giovanni Bellini, Mantegna, Correggio, Titian, Lorenzo Lotto, Tintoretto and Tiepolo. Local Lombard artists Foppa and Bergognone, and Leonardo's disciples Boltraffio and Sodoma, are also represented.

Over in the **Rocchetta**, once the Palazzo's guards' room and where the inhabitants of the castle hid in times of seige, are fine Egyptian and archaeological collections, as well as ceramics and furniture.

Parco Sempione

Behind the Castello, the Sforza family's old hunting grounds were transformed at the end of the 19th century into public gardens carefully laid out as an English landscaped park, **Parco Sempione** (open daily 6.30am–8pm, later in summer).

The pace here is leisurely, away from the brisk bustle of the centre. In the right-hand corner of Parco Sempione is an **aquarium** of exotic tropical fish. Over on the left side of the park is the **Palazzo del Arte**, a thoroughly modern exhibition hall, most noted for the world-famous *Triennale* show of decorative arts.

A fine **equestrian statue** by Francesco Barzagli in the middle of the park commemorates Napoleon III's passage through the neoclassical **Arco della Pace** at the far end of the park, after the Italian-French victory over the Austrians in 1859 *(see page 20)*. The triumphal arch, completed in 1838 is the starting point of the Corso Sempione, the Simplon Road that Napoleon Bonaparte ordered to be built through the Alps – according to local belief, the pass influenced local climatic conditions by creating a hole in the hitherto protective Alpine barrier.

Fun for all the family at Parco Sempione

THE BRERA

Milan's bohemian yet chic Brera, just a short walk east of the Castello Sforzesco, is the city's traditional artisan area. Quiet in the day, except for activities in its handful of boutiques, galleries and cafés, the Brera picks up at night, when the locals stroll along its pedestrian streets. The area houses one of Italy's most prestigious art collections, the Pinacoteca di Brera.

Pinacoteca di Brera

The main artery through the area is Via Brera, home to the **Pinacoteca di Brera** (open Tues–Sun 8.30am–7pm), contained within a handsome 17th-century Jesuit palace. In its fine arcaded courtyard, notice a bronze statue of Napoleon – a remarkable, rare example of the emperor without clothes. (The marble original is at Apsley House in London.) Homage is paid here to Napoleon Bonaparte for turning the Brera into a national gallery with the art he confiscated from the Church and recalcitrant nobles. Most of what he expropriated in Italy for the Louvre in Paris ended up back in Milan at the Brera after Waterloo.

Among the highlights of the gallery are: paintings by Giovanni Bellini of the

Francesco Hayez's *The Kiss*

Madonna and Child and an exquisitely personal *Pietà*; two Titian portraits, *Antonio Porcia* and *St Jerome*; Veronese's *Jesus in the Garden*; Tintoretto's dramatic *Discovery of St Mark's Body*; and an impressive *Jesus at the Column* by the many-talented Donato Bramante.

St Sebastian

Andrea Mantegna's works include a touching *Madonna* and a startling, peculiarly foreshortened *Dead Christ*. Pieces by Piero della Francesca include his celebrated *Montefeltro Altarpiece* (1474), his last work. The ethereal beauty of Correggio's *Nativity* and *Adoration of the Magi* and Raphael's stately *Betrothal of the Madonna* contrast with the earthier inspiration of Caravaggio's *Supper at Emmaus*.

Lombard masters include Bergognone, Boltraffio, Foppa and Luini, while the non-Italian artists represented include El Greco, Rubens, Van Dyck and Rembrandt. The modern collection has notable works by Modigliani, Boccioni, de Chirico, Carrà and de Pisis. Proudly displayed at the end of the tour is *The Kiss*, a sentimental work by Francesco Hayez, former director of the Brera.

Brera Churches

After visiting the Palazzo di Brera, cross Via Brera and walk down Via del Carmine. On your right is the imposing church of **Santa Maria del Carmine** (Mon–Fri 7.15–11.30am and 3.30–7pm, Sat and Sun till 7.30pm). Nearby, on Piazza San Marco, is **San Marco** (Mon–Sat 7am–noon, 4–7pm, Sun

7am–1pm); with a length of 95m (315ft), this is Milan's second largest church after the Duomo. Also in the area, on Piazza Crociate, is **San Simpliciano** (Mon–Fri 7am–noon and 3–7pm, Sat and Sun 8am–noon and 4–7pm), one of the most beautiful churches in Milan, believed to have been founded by St Ambrose in the 4th century.

The Artistic Quarter

Once you've sated your yearning for culture by visiting the galleries and churches of the Brera, it may be time to wind down and indulge yourself with some shopping or window-shopping in the district's ultra-stylish boutiques. On Via Solferino, you'll find one-off clothes stores (mostly for women) and a scattering of cool shoe shops, showcasing the designer heels for which Milan is famed; purchasing such footwear and actually managing to tread the city's cobbled streets in them are two different matters, however. The cobbled **Via Fiori Chiari** has some designer boutiques and small commercial art galleries, but these sit side by side with bars and cafés, where you can relax for a while and soak up the local atmosphere. On summer evenings, this street comes alive as the Milanese undertake their *passeggiata*, or evening stroll, and street-vendors try their hardest to sell fake Louis Vuitton and Prada bags. Note that on the third Saturday of the month, a lively antiques market spills on to Via Fiori Chiari.

Legend has it that on 29 May 1176, the day of the Battle of Legnano (*see page 13*), three white doves flew out of the room in San Simpliciano where the relics of the three martyrs were kept. They landed on the flagpoles and spurred on the communes to victory. In commemoration, balloons are released on 29 May every year in the square in front of the church.

Designer labels dominate Montenapoleone

NORTHEAST OF THE DUOMO

Montenapoleone and San Babila are among the wealthiest areas in Milan. Come here for back-to-back designer labels, smart *palazzi* and two notable museums: the Museo Poldi Pezzoli and the Museo di Milano. As you head northeast, you reach Milan's second main green space, the Gardini Pubblici, and, further north still, the Cimiterio Monumentale.

Quadrilatero della Moda

Only a few select shopping districts in the world achieve the status of monuments, and right up there with London's Bond Street, New York's Fifth Avenue, Los Angeles's Rodeo Drive, and Paris's rue du Faubourg St Honoré, is Milan's **Via Montenapoleone** (referred to in some guidebooks as 'Montenapo', although locals rarely use the nickname). This glamorous street is one side of Milan's *quadrilatero della moda* (fashion quadrilateral), also incorporating vias Mazoni, Sant'Andrea and della Spiga. Reached north of the Piazza La Scala along Via Alessandro Manzoni, the Montenapoleone neighbourhood is a veritable living exhibition of Milan's exquisite sense of modern and classical design at its very polished. Fashion, jewellery, furniture and luxurious household accessories are all on dazzling show along Via Montenapoleone and Via della Spiga. Countless shops of equal pedigree have long spilled over onto the web of narrow streets between them. Ladies who shop don't miss an afternoon respite at the historic Bar Cova – ask for their renowned house cocktail, the *aperitivo Cova*.

This is Italy's finest window shopping, amid a setting of elegant 18th-century palazzi housing deluxe boutiques with theatrical window displays that are works of art in themselves. Beyond the predominantly warm, yellow tones of the façades, explore the beautiful inner courtyards, which are wonderful havens of peace away from the city bustle. Nearby, everybody rushes on Via Bagutta, with its famous bistro that shares the same name *(see page 137)*, and along Via Sant'Andrea, Via Gesù, Via Verri, Via Santo Spirito and Via Borgospessi.

Prada of Milan

Established in Milan in 1913 by Mario Prada, the family firm of Fratelli Prada started by crafting luxury leather goods for the rich and famous. Mario's granddaughter, Miuccia, inherited the business in 1978. Although unschooled in fashion design – she has a PhD in political science – Miuccia has taken the firm from strength to strength. She has expanded into mens- and womenswear, producing universally acclaimed collections dominated by clean, almost stark, lines and hip, yet subtle, decoration. She introduced a more affordable line under her nickname, Miu Miu, opening the market for Prada goods even further.

Museo Poldi Pezzoli

Just north of Piazza della Scala is the **Museo Poldi Pezzoli** (Via Alessandro Manzoni 12; open Tues–Sun 10am–6pm), the former home and art collection of the nobleman Gian Giacomo Poldi Pezzoli (1822–79), left to the city as an art foundation on his death. The collection contains a number of splendid paintings, but also antique watches, sundials, Murano glass and fine 16th-century Persian carpets, as well as soldiers' chain mail and face armour.

Armani, Milan

Among its prodigious collection of painted masterpieces are a Giovanni Bellini *Pietà*, Piero della Francesca's *San Nicola da Toledano*, Mantegna's *Madonna and Child*, a Botticelli *Madonna*, Antonio Pollaiuoli's lovely *Portrait of a Young Woman* and major works by Palma il Vecchio, Filippo Lippi, Perugino, Lorenzo Lotto, Tiepolo and the Lombard masters.

Museo di Milano

The municipal museum, or **Museo di Milano** (open Tues–Sun 9am–1pm, 2–6pm), on Via Sant'Andrea 6, in the 18th-century Palazzo Morando, traces the city's history through a series of paintings, drawings and prints. The specific history of Italy's independence movement in the 19th century is recounted in the **Museo del Risorgimento** (open

Tues–Sun 9.30am–5.30pm), on Via Borgonuovo 23. The museum houses a collection of works from the mid-7th century up to 1870. Included is an important collection of flags, decorations of the crowning of Napoleon I as king of Italy as well as some works by Giuseppe Mazzini.

Giardini Pubblici

Just north of the city centre, the private gardens of the 18th-century aristocracy have been transformed into a lovely 17-hectare (42-acre) public park. Wide avenues of chestnut trees criss-cross handsome landscaped gardens in the classical Italian style amidst rock banks and ponds. For children, there are pony-carts, a miniature train and bumper cars.

Inside the park, the classical French-style **Villa Reale**, built in 1790 for the Belgioioso family, contains the **Civica Galleria d'Arte Moderna** (Modern Art Gallery; open Tues–Sun 9am–5.30pm). You will find work by Italian futurists including Boccioni, Carrà and Balla, sculpture by Marino Marini, and paintings by French 19th-century artists from Corot, Sisley, Manet, Cézanne and Gauguin to Van Gogh.

The **Museo Civico di Storia Naturale** (Natural History Museum; open Mon–Fri 9am–6pm, Sat and Sun 9.30am–6.30pm), the largest in Italy, has a great collection of minerals, giant crystals, insects, fossils and dinosaurs, as well as a library. Alternatively, you can always reach for the stars at the nearby **Planetario di Milano** (Planetarium). On the far west side of the park, in the Palazzo Dugnani, the **Museo del Cinema** (Cinema Museum) shows old cameras, projectors and, best of all, films.

Cimitero Monumentale

Not everyone thinks of a cemetery as a place to go sightseeing. This particular resting-place, however, is well worth the 15-minute taxi ride northwest of the Duomo for its amazing

Flowers and statuary at the Cimitero Monumentale

tributes in granite and marble to bourgeois Milanese pride and pathos. When they say *monumentale*, they are not joking. A Pharaonic pyramid, enormous Roman sarcophagus, lifesize crucifixion and several other morbid but fascinating tributes vie for your attention. Nothing, it seems, is too good for the dearly departed Milanese. The centrepiece is a gigantic Neo-Gothic temple sheltering the tomb of famous novelist Alessandro Manzoni, author of *I promessi sposi (The Betrothed),* along with busts of the revered Verdi – who wrote his *Requiem* in honour of Manzoni – and independence heroes Giuseppe Garibaldi and Camilo Cavour.

Soldiers are particularly well served, including a colonel sculpted with all his medals and a sergeant major being devoured by a Gorgon. Best of all is one Davide Campari who, before he died, commissioned a full-size reproduction of Leonardo's *The Last Supper* for his tomb. The guardians are usually pleased to show you where.

WESTERN MILAN

Leonardo spent 18 years in the service of Duke Ludovico Sforza *(see page 17)*, and several monuments testify to the artist's presence in the city. From the west side of the Castello Sforzesco (Metro: Cadorna), you are within easy walking distance of two monuments which demonstrate the different sides of Leonardo da Vinci's genius. His acclaimed artistic masterpiece, *The Last Supper,* is housed in the old Dominican monastery *(see page 52)*, and his scientific inventions in the Museo della Scienza e della Tecnica (Science and Technology Museum; *see page 53*). The church of Sant'

Leonardo's *The Last Supper showing, from left to right: Bartholomew, James the Lesser, Andrew, Judas Iscariot, Peter, John, Jesus, Thomas, James the Elder, Philip, Matthew, Thaddeus and Simon*

Ambrogio, Milan's most venerated place of worship, is conveniently situated nearby.

Santa Maria delle Grazie

Even without Leonardo da Vinci's painting in the adjoining building, the church of **Santa Maria delle Grazie** (on Piazza Santa Maria della Grazia) is a jewel of Renaissance architecture. A restoration of the church's interior has been underway since 2001. Adding to an earlier Gothic design, in 1492 Donato Bramante – Pope Julius II's chief architect in Rome – fashioned a magnificent red-brick-and-white-stone **chancel** *(tribuna)* towering over the rear of the church. The graceful lines of the rectangular choir and 16-sided cupola are best viewed from the little **cloister** that Bramante built on the north side. Once inside the church, which was originally conceived as the Sforza family's burial place (the tombs of Ludovico il Moro and his wife Beatrice are to be restored to their rightful place here), stand in the choir to appreciate the full majesty of the chancel's dome. Notice, too, the exquisite inlaid wood and carving of the prayer stalls in the apse.

➤ After being painstakingly restored recently, Leonardo da Vinci's **The Last Supper** (*Il Cenacolo*, 1498) is on view once again on one of the walls of the little Dominican refectory to the left of the church. Despite centuries of deterioration and a number of clumsy restorations since it was completed, the painting still carries enormous psychological impact. In the moment Leonardo has chosen to capture in his painting, we see the trauma of each of the disciples following Jesus' declaration: 'One of you will betray me.'

Almost as awe-inspiring as the painting itself is the painstaking recovery of the fragmentary but still powerful traces of the 'real Leonardo.' The recent restoration reveals, for example, that Philip has an expression of acute grief, not the simpering pathos left by past 'restorers' who presumed to improve on the original. Since this is one of Milan's principal sights, booking at least three days in advance is essential (tel: 02-89421146).

On the wall opposite, the superb condition of Donato da Montorfano's *Crucifixion* (dating from 1495) shows how much better preserved Leonardo's work would have been if only he had - accepted the constraints of fresco – he experimented with the technique on *The Last Supper*, thus lessening the work's durability.

Santa Maria delle Grazie

Museo della Scienza e della Tecnica

For the other, equally fascinating aspect of Leonardo's
talents visit the **Museo della
Scienza e della Tecnica**
(Science and Technology
Museum) in the nearby Via
San Vittore. Among the
rooms devoted to scientific
history, one gallery is reserved for Leonardo's inventions. They are displayed as
models, constructed from
details in his notebooks. You
will see his aircraft, a machine for making screws, a

**Architectural detail, Museo
della Scienza e della Tecnica**

revolving bridge, an hydraulic timber-cutter, some machine-
tools, and a system of map-making by aerial views long before any aircraft, even his own, had become operational.

The Basilico di Sant'Ambrogio

At the eastern end of Via San Vittore is Milan's most revered
sanctuary, the **Basilico di Sant'Ambrogio** (open daily
7am–noon, 2–7pm). Dedicated to the city's patron saint, the
current basilica was built between the 9th and 12th centuries
and stands on the site of a church built in AD 386 under Aurelius Ambrosius, first Bishop of Milan. Its position, next to
the Catholic University, honours the scholarship of the man
who left a revered personal legacy of hymns and philosophi-
cal homilies, so convincingly sweet with his words that his
name gave us the word 'ambrosia'.

The sober, five-bayed façade is characteristic Lombard
Romanesque, flanked by a 9th-century campanile on the

right and a taller 12th-century tower to the left, and topped by a modern loggia.

In the interior, to the left of the rib-vaulted nave, notice the 11th-century **pulpit** standing over a Christian sarcophagus of the Roman era. In the north (left) aisle are Bergognone's painting of *Jesus the Redeemer* and Bernardino Luini's *Madonna*, in the south (right) aisle, frescoes by Tiepolo. The **high altar**, covered in gold and silver and richly embedded with precious stones, stands beneath a 9th-century canopy carved with Byzantine-Romanesque reliefs. The remains of St Ambrose himself are buried in the **crypt** beneath the presbytery at the far-east end of the church.

The basilica's museum, the **Museo della Basilica di Sant' Ambrogio** (open Wed–Mon 10am–noon and 3–5pm; Sat and Sun 3–5pm), containing treasures amassed over centuries and relics that date back to the basilica's earliest times, was recently rehoused in the Museo Diocesano and the San Vittore

---

Milan's Patron Saint

Aurelius Ambrosius (c. AD334 or 340–397) was a no-nonsense bishop. Born of Christian parents but with no religious training, this Roman civil servant responded to his unexpected appointment by taking a crash course in theology. He was willing to 'render unto Caesar' but not to let Caesar ride roughshod over his ideas of God. After his studies convinced him of the evil of Arianism (a then-popular belief denying that Jesus was consubstantial with God), he refused the demand of Emperor Valentinian to hand over one of Milan's churches to the Arians. Emperor Theodosius I conceded, but when he then massacred thousands of rebels in Thessalonica, Ambrosius not only excommunicated him but also made him come to Milan and prostrate himself in penance at the cathedral. Of Theodosius, Ambrosius said: 'The emperor is within the church; he is not above it.'

in Ciel d'Oro, with some works in the Antico Oratorio della Passione (Piazza Sant' Ambrogio 23a).

In the middle of the Piazza Sant'Ambrogio is the Tempio della Vittoria (1928, by Muzio), commemorating the Milanese who fell during World War I. At the southern end of the square is the Colonna del Diavolo, an antique column, which derives its name from a local legend. You will notice two holes in the column, and it is said that they were left by the devil's horns when he was angered at his discovery that St Ambrose was not to be tempted.

Capella della Santa Sevina, Sant'Ambrogio

Corso Magento Museums

Situated on Corso Magento 15, the **Museo Archeologico** (Archaeological Museum; open Tues–Sun 9am–5.30pm) harbours a collection of Greek, Etruscan and Roman antiquities in the former 16th-century Monastero Maggiore (entrance is through the cloisters). In the monastery's lay chapel there are several frescoes by artist Bernardino Luini.

Also on Corso Magento, at No 71, is the **Museo Teatrale** (Opera Museum; open daily 9am–6pm), formerly housed in a building adjacent to La Scala but relocated in 2002 to Palazzo Busca. The museum traces the fascinating history of opera and theatre in the city, with memorabilia of composers including Verdi, Bellini and Donizetti on show.

Reflections along the canals

THE NAVIGLI

Once a modest but colourful working-class neighbourhood on the south side of town, the *Navigli* – or canal – district has become a re-gentrified neighbourhood and is hugely popular for its prodigious bars, trendy bistros, open-air cafés, boutiques, galleries, artists' studios and several open-air markets.

Two canals start out from the **Darsena basin** near the sprawling Piazza XXIV Maggio (where a pompous arch celebrates Napoleon III's victory over the Austrians at Marengo; *see page 20*). The **Naviglio Grande** runs west out to Abbiategrasso, and the **Naviglio Pavese** south to Pavia. They were originally dug in the Middle Ages to bring agricultural products into the city from the fertile plains, and by the 17th century they also served the gentry as waterways to their country villas.

From May to mid-September guided cruises are offered on the Naviglio Grande; for more details, contact the Milan

Tourist Office *(see page 128)*. A popular local festival is held along the *Darsena Ticinese* on the first Sunday in June *(see page 95)*.

San Lorenzo Maggiore

The church of San Lorenzo Maggiore is situated near the ancient **Porta Ticinese** and the **Colonne di San Lorenzo**, 16 Corinthian columns from a temple portico, which comprise Milan's only substantial Roman remains. (They are believed to have once formed part of either a Roman temple or a complex of thermal baths dating from the 2nd or 3rd century AD, and they were placed here in the 4th century to form a grand entrance portico to the church beyond. With its late 19th-century façade, the current Romanesque church, the **Basilica di San Lorenzo Maggiore**, stands on the site of an early Christian church. To mark that era is a striking bronze statue (recast) of Emperor Constantine.

San Lorenzo's outstanding feature, on the south (right) side, is the octagonal **Capella di Sant'Aquilino** built in the 4th century as an imperial mausoleum. Inside are 5th-century mosaics of Jesus, the Apostles and Elijah, an early Christian sarcophagus and various notable Roman architectural fragments.

Canal History

Until the 1970s, Milan was Italy's third-largest port in terms of tonnage, and barges carrying sand and gravel travelled into the city along the canals. The Naviglio Grande, which leads more than 50km (30 miles) to the River Ticino, was built in the 14th century. The Naviglio Pavese, built by the Visconti family and measuring 33km (20 miles), saw more then 1,400 barges travel along its narrow strip each year.

Sant'Eustorgio

Sant'Eustorgio

A park, **Parco delle Basiliche**, stretches south of San Lorenzo Maggiore down to the medieval **Basilica di Sant'Eustorgio** (open daily 7.30am–noon, 3.30–6.30pm). Work on the basilica began in the 11th century on the site of an oratory founded by Bishop Eustorgius (and, according to legend, containing the relics of the Three Magi, presented to the bishop by the Emperor Constantine). The building was harmoniously expanded over the next 400 years, with notable additions including the fine **campanile** and the **Capella Portinari**, a jewel of Renaissance architecture. The chapel is dedicated to St Peter the Martyr, a 13th-century inquisitor murdered by one of his victims and honoured here with masterly frescoes (1468) by Vincenzo Foppa.

Just as impressive is the St Peter's **tomb** sculpted by Giovanni di Balduccio in 1339. Off the south (right) transept, the huge Roman sarcophagus in the **Chapel of the Magi** held the relics of the three kings until 1164, when they were moved to Cologne, Germany.

Santa Maria presso San Celso

East of Sant'Eustorgio, on Corso Italia, is **Santa Maria presso San Celso**, a Romanesque church with a 10th-century bell-tower. Visit it on a bright day, in order to view Paris Bordone's beautiful *Holy Family with St Jerome* and 14th-century frescoes in the south (right) aisle, as well as the handsome inlaid-wood **choir stalls**. In the north (left) aisle is Bergognone's *Jesus in the Stable*.

DAY TRIPS FROM MILAN

Although the towns of Pavia, Monza and Bergamo can all be reached on easy day trips from Milan, they also make for good overnight trips. Bergamo, in particular, is a very pleasant stopover on the way to or from Lake Garda.

Certosa di Pavia

After Milan's Duomo, this great charterhouse, the **Certosa di Pavia** (open Tues–Sun 9–11.30am, 2.30–4.30pm; 6pm in summer, 4pm in winter; a monk conducts tours of the building; a small tip is expected), begun in the 15th century as a Visconti family mausoleum, is the most spectacular monument in the region. A 30-minute drive south of Milan, it can be visited independently of Pavia itself, which lies 7km (4 miles) further down the road.

The Certosa di Pavia

In 1947 Cistercian monks took over the running of Pavia's great charterhouse from the Carthusians. They have, however, continued the traditional manufacture of herbal liqueurs.

Beyond the public entrance, the interior courtyard leading to the church has **wine cellars** and **food stores**, which you'll find located across from the Baroque **Palazzo Ducale**, which constitutes the prior's and ducal apartments.

For the construction and decoration of the monastery's church, Duke Gian Galeazzo Visconti used many of the masons and sculptors who were working on his cathedral in Milan. The edifice marks a crucial point in the transition in styles from flamboyant Gothic to Renaissance. Even without the originally designed crowning gable, the sculpted marble façade has a dazzling impact. There are more than 70 statues of prophets, saints and apostles above the medallion reliefs of Roman emperors.

The Gothic interior, with its characteristic vaulting, is lightened with brightly coloured pavements. Among the chapels, which were decorated in Baroque style in the late 16th century, notice in the north (left) aisle an exquisite Perugino altarpiece of *God the Father*. Right of the triumphant Baroque high altar are a finely carved 15th-century *lavabo* (ritual basin) and a delightful *Madonna and Child* by Luini. In the south (right) transept is the **Visconti tomb**. The **Great Cloister**, also to the south, has 122 arches, with similar terracotta decoration for the monks' 24 cells. Their **refectory** has ceiling frescoes by Bergognone.

Pavia

The Lombards' first capital is now a sleepy, red-bricked university town (population 85,000), some 34 km (21 miles) south of Milan. Hurry through its modern suburbs to the attractive *centro storico*. The Lombard kings established their court in Pavia in the 6th century *(see page 12)*; French King Charlemagne was crowned Emperor here in 774, Frederick Barbarossa in 1155. Pavia was the birthplace (c.1005) of Lanfranc, first Archbishop of Canterbury under the Normans. The French have less happy memories of the city, since King François I was captured by Emperor Charles V in 1525 at the crucial battle of Pavia (in the northern outskirts at Mirabello) and imprisoned in Madrid.

The Spanish ramparts from the 17th century are visible along the northern edge of the city centre as you drive in from Milan. Start walking on the south side of town at the **Ponte Coperto** (Covered Bridge), which spans the Ticino river. The bridge has been reconstructed east of the medieval original, which was bombed in 1944. The Ticino descends from Switzerland via Lake Maggiore to join the Po southeast of Pavia.

The university town of Pavia

From the picturesque riverside road, take the Via Diacono towards the church of **San Michele**, the city's major Romanesque monument. The church's octagonal dome was completed in 1155 for Emperor Frederick Barbarossa's crowning, and the church was the site for all coronations thereafter. The simple sandstone façade is

Ancient houses in Pavia

notable for its subtly sculpted friezes over the three recessed portals and an elegant band of 21 arches following the angle of the roof gable. The interior has superb rib vaulting over the nave and aisles and fine carving on the column capitals.

Head left on Corso Garibaldi and turn right along Strada Nuova, which traces the old Roman road's south–north axis from the Ponte Coperto. Behind the *Broletto* (town hall) is the late-15th-century **Duomo**, a Renaissance structure with details added by Bramante and Leonardo da Vinci. The dome dates from the 19th century, but the façade was not completed until later, in 1933.

Back on Strada Nuova, cross the ancient Roman east–west axis (now Corso Mazzini and Corso Cavour), to pass the 18th-century buildings of the **University of Pavia**, on the right. The university was originally founded by the Lombards as the nation's foremost school of law, and was made a full university by the Visconti in 1361. Pavia's most celebrated teacher was Alessandro Volta (1745–1827), professor of physics and pioneer in electricity who gave his name to the unit of electric measurement. Napoleon bestowed on him the title of count.

A well conceived **museum** recounts the fascinating history of the university. On Piazza Leonardo da Vinci are three medieval **tower houses** of the Pavia nobility and beneath the square the 11th-century **crypt** of Sant' Eusebio.

At the north end of Strada Nuova is the Visconti's formidable 14th-century fortress, **Castello Visconteo**. Its back section was lost in 1527, but there are two corner turrets remaining on the south side. Enter the fine terracotta arcaded courtyard for access to the **Museo Civico**. Besides a small but interesting collection of Roman antiquities and Lombard sculpture, the **Pinacoteca** houses important numerous works by Giovanni Bellini, Correggio, Boltraffio, Foppa, Tiepolo and the Netherlands painters Hugo Van der Goes and Lucas Van Leyden.

Over to the west (at the end of Via Griziotti) is the 12th-century church of **San Pietro in Ciel d'Oro**. It is revered as the last resting place of St Augustine, whose relics are said to have been brought here from Carthage (near where he died in 430) and are now enshrined in the great Gothic, sculpted marble **Arca di Sant'Agostino** (1362). The Romanesque interior provides a simple setting for the grandiose monument. The *Ciel d'Oro* (golden ceiling) of the church's name refers to a now long-gone gilded vault. A verse from Dante's *Paradiso* is quoted on the façade in reference to the martyred Roman poet Boethius, who is buried in the crypt.

Monza

If you do not feel like driving through Milan's northeast industrial suburbs, it's an easy 30-minute bus ride from beside *Stazione Centrale* to this picturesque gingerbread town with a population of 120,000. Monza, now the fabled home of

Monza

Grand Prix motor racing *(see also page 94)*, was actually founded on hat and carpet manufacturing.

The track and grandstands take up some 15 percent of the lovely **Villa Reale park**, which covers 800 hectares (2,000 acres) in all. The land was confiscated from the aristocracy and handed over to the people in 1805 by Napoleon's stepson and viceroy in Italy, Eugène de Beauharnais. The English-style landscaped parkland is still dotted with patrician mansions and is home to the Austrian Archduke Ferdinand's neoclassical Villa Reale (1780), set among rose gardens and greenhouses.

This is great picnic country and caters to all forms of sport: tennis, golf (Milan Golf Club has 18- and 9-hole courses), polo, field hockey, swimming, skating, hiking and jogging. Bicycles can also be rented in the park. Wild stag, hare and pheasant roam freely, some all the way on to the woodlands in the middle of the racetrack. Horse races were held at the Mirabello hippodrome until it fell into disrepair.

Historically, Monza was an important city of the Lombard kings. The Gothic **cathedral** is older than Milan's, and is notable for its 13th-century white-and-green marble façade and Pellegrino Tibaldi's brick campanile (1605). The church was founded in AD595 by the Lombard Queen Theodolinda, whose tomb is in the **Capella Zavattari** to the left of the high altar. Inside the church's **Museo Serpero** downstairs is the Lombards' **Iron Crown**, used in the coronation both of Holy Roman Emperors and Napoleon himself. It is so called because it is said to contain a piece of iron from one of the nails used to hammer Jesus to the cross. Theodolinda's treasure also includes ancient silver, ivory, embroidery, silk and other religious relics.

Bergamo

Rising out of the plain of the Po valley around its own steep little hill, roughly 47km (30 miles) northeast of Milan, the delightful town of **Bergamo** makes a welcome break from the monotony of the *autostrada*. Divided into lower and upper cities (*Città Bassa* and *Alta* respectively), the population of around 125,000 earns a living from fabric manufacturing and the metal industry. The town has a proud soldiering history, having given the Venetian Republic a famous *condottiere,* Bartolomeo Colleoni, and the largest contingent in Garibaldi's 1,000 Red Shirts for the *Risorgimento (see page 20)*. A funicular links the two parts of the city along with a winding road, but it is advisable to leave your car behind, as parking is limited.

Città Bassa

The Lower City is the modern town of shops, hotels and restaurants serving local specialities such as *polenta e osei*, creamy corn porridge and roasted local birds. Marcello Piacentini creatively laid out the area with style and panache in the early 20th century along airy, broad boulevards and squares, before he succumbed to the demands of Mussolini as official architect of the Fascist State.

The main street, Viale Giovanni XXIII, leads to Piazza Matteotti and the hub of the town's lively café scene along the tree-lined **Sentierone** arcades. Opposite is the 18th-century **Teatro Donizetti** and a monument showing the Bergamo-born opera composer accompanied by the naked lady he is always said to have needed for inspiration.

At the eastern end of the piazza, step inside the church of **San Bartolomeo** to look at Lorenzo Lotto's fine altar painting (1516). Climbing to the Upper City, further east, **Via Pignolo** is most notable for its elegant 16th- to 18th-century *palazzi* and the church of **Santo Spirito**, with a fine polyptych by Bergognone.

Santa Maria Maggiore crowns the Città Alta

Città Alta

The recently restructured Venetian walls, which can be toured from above or within a series of secret passageways, still protect the historic Upper City on the 366-m (1,200-ft) hill. 'Alta,' meaning 'high', refers to the city's altitude, 400m (1,300ft) above sea level. The gracious **Piazza Vecchia** is surrounded by several grand Renaissance public edifices – notably the **Palazzo della Ragione** with a medieval tower, Torre del Comune. Take the lift to enjoy the rooftop view over the Po valley to the Alps.

The town's most venerable edifice, situated on Piazza del Duomo, is the 12th-century Romanesque church

Bergamo's famous sons include Donizetti, arguably the most important composer of the 1830s. There is a monument to him on Piazza Cavour, adjacent to the theatre named in his honour.

of **Santa Maria Maggiore**. Notice the finely carved, monumental porch and the elegant, slender campanile. The Baroque interior has impressive 16th-century **tapestries** and Donizetti's tomb on the west wall. The inlaid **choir stalls** and intarsia on the altar rail include designs by Lorenzo Lotto. Also note the beautiful wooden confessional by Andrea Fantoni.

Adjacent to the church is the Renaissance **Capella Colleoni** (Colleoni Chapel), the *condottiere*'s extravagant mausoleum in red, white and green marble. The lavish façade illustrating classical and Biblical allegory is no masterpiece, but it gives wonderful expression to the old soldier's legendary *braggadocio*. Some of the windows' pillars reproduce the shape of cannon barrels that Colleoni pioneered on the battlefield. Inside is his tomb, a gilded wooden equestrian statue and ceiling frescoes by Tiepolo.

A short walk from the Città Alta's Porta Sant'Agostino, the recently restructured **Galleria dell'Accademia Carrara** stands on the northeast side of the Lower City. It includes a *Madonna and Child* by Mantegna, and paintings by Bellini, Lotto, Raphael, Titian, Botticelli and Carpaccio. Among the foreign artists represented are Holbein, Rubens, Velázquez, Rembrandt and El Greco. In front of the Galleria is a **Modern Art Museum**, built in 2000.

WHERE TO GO: THE LAKES

Italy's most famous lakes – Maggiore, Varese, Como and Garda – are all within easy reach of Milan. A popular destination with the Italians themselves, they are at their best, and busiest, in spring, when the luxuriant vegetation is in full bloom. In summer a trip here makes a refreshing change from the intense city heat of Milan.

LAKE MAGGIORE

Blessed with a temperate, mild climate and luxuriant vegetation, Lake Maggiore is a watery arm curving along the foot of the Alps, 65 km (40 miles) long and nearly 5 km (3 miles) at its widest point, with the 'elbow' at Baveno. With the Ticino river as its main affluent, it covers 210 sq km (80 sq miles), one fifth of it being at the Locarno (northern) end, in Switzerland. Since 1748, the west shore has been part of the Piedmont region, but it has never lost its identity as part of Lombardy since the domination of the Visconti in the Middle Ages and the presence of the Borromeo family from the 15th century. The family dynasty, which gave Milan its greatest cardinals, also gave its name to the lake's romantic islands – the Isole Borromee, or Borromean Islands. These are still owned by the family, as are the lake's fishing rights. Trains from Milan's *Stazione Nord* take one hour to Arona on the lake's southern shore or 90 minutes to Laveno on the eastern side.

Stresa

Since the 19th century, and particularly since the construction of Napoleon's Simplon Road through the Alps, Stresa has been the lake's principal resort, home to a number of

Varenna waterside

luxurious hotels. The lakeside **Lungolago promenade** is famous for its flowers and bewitching views of the islands. On the southern outskirts, in the **Villa Pallavicino** (1850), visit the beautiful, hillside botanical gardens that occupy sprawling parkland laid out in English, French and Italian style.

You can also take the cable car up to the peak of the **Mottarone** (at a vertiginously high 1,491m/4,892 ft), from where there are exhilarating views of the Lombardy lakes, the Alps and the Po valley. Alternatively, a free piece of the toll road will get you there via the **Giardino Alpinia** (Alpine Gardens), displaying an impressive 2,000 varieties of mountain plants.

Palms in Baveno, a pretty resort between Stresa and Verbania

Baveno

North of Stresa, this quiet - little resort was visited by Queen Victoria, who promenaded here when staying at the nearby Castello Bianco. Baveno is famous for its local red-and-white granite used in the construction of St Peter's basilica in Rome. The octagonal, Renaissance **baptistery** on the main square and the 12th-century **parish church** are both worth a look.

Verbania

Just around the 'elbow' of Lake Maggiore from Stresa, this handsome resort shares, along with neighbouring **Pallanza** and **Intra**, a microclimate of hot summers and gloriously mild winters that support a carefully nurtured, semi-tropical vegetation. The town takes its name from the vervain tea herb that grows rampant here (as do fragrant magnolias).

Just north of Verbania with a direct service by boat, **Villa Taranto** offers the lake's most spectacular **botanical gardens** (open Apr–Oct). The 16 hectares (40 acres) of parkland were bequeathed to Italy in 1931 by Scottish soldier Captain Neil McEacharn. Among the fountains, waterfalls, basins and lily ponds, you will find several thousand varieties of plants. They have been brought to these gardens from all over the world and gradually acclimatised here over the years. This is the only place apart from the Nile valley where some Egyptian plants will grow.

Isole Borromee

Close to the western shore of Lake Maggiore are the **Isole Borromee** (Borromean Islands), named after the noble Italian family who bought them in the 16th century. Celebrated for their Baroque *palazzi* and magnificent gardens, the islands are all within easy reach by boat from Stresa, Baveno or Pallanza.

Isola Bella

Isola Bella is named after Isabella, wife of Count Carlo Borromeo, who planned the island haven for her. The soil in its ten tiers of terraced gardens had to be brought by barge from the mainland. In addition to admirable works by Annibale Carracci, Tiepolo, Zuccarelli and Giordano, the 17th-century *palazzo* is decorated with landscape paintings by Antonio Tempesta, who used the island as a refuge after being accused of murdering his wife. There is a wonderful collection of 18th-century puppets in the basement. The terraced gardens constitute one of the finest examples of the

White peacock, Isola Madre

Italian formal style. View the lake from the uppermost terrace, by the unicorn statue that is the Borromeo family emblem.

Isola dei Pescatori

With a name meaning Fishermen's Island, **Isola dei Pescatori** is, indeed, simply a peaceful fishing village with tiny, narrow streets and several pleasant little restaurants that make for a pleasant lunch stop.

Isola Madre

Further out in the lake is **Isola Madre**, the largest of the islands. The **botanical gardens** set around the 16th-century *palazzo* here are renowned for their rhododendrons, camellias (April) and azaleas (May), as well as resident pheasants and raucous white peacocks all year round.

Locarno and Ascona (Switzerland)

Don't forget your passport if you intend to cross the border into the Swiss part of the lake. (The last town on the Italian side, Cannobio, is famous for its anti-smuggling flotilla of *torpediere* boats.) Locarno is one of the very few places in the Alpine country where you can see unlikely subtropical foliage such as banana plants, date palms and orange trees.

Milan's lords once holidayed on these very shores, as is testified by the handsome remains of the **Castello Visconti**. Its 15th-century courtyard, surrounded by graceful arcades, leads to the **Museo Civico**, which harbours a rich archeological collection that includes many notable Roman relics.

A few streets away is the airy, curving **Piazza Grande**, the city's main square. Its arcades offset Locarno's annual International Film Festival, during which films are shown on an outdoor screen.

Uphill from the Piazza is the **Città Vecchia**, the old town of stately villas, timeworn apartment buildings, hidden gardens and venerable churches. Among the turreted mansions, look out for **Casa Rusca** in Piazza Sant'Antonio, containing the art collection donated by French-born sculptor Jean Arp, a founder of the Dada Movement and leading Surrealist, who died here in 1966.

Ascona is separated from Locarno by the Maggia river flowing into the lake. Once a simple fishing village, it has become popular with artists and writers. Favoured in the past by dancer Isadora Duncan, painter Paul Klee, and

Crossing Lake Maggiore

the exiled Lenin, it now hosts frequent art exhibitions and an annual festival of classical music. The **lake promenade** has lively outdoor cafés, bars and restaurants, while numerous Swiss jewellery shops and Italian fashion boutiques pepper the side streets.

Santa Caterina del Sasso

Prized frescoes in the church of Santa Caterina del Sasso

Along the eastern shore of the lake, not far from the tiny village of Reno, is **Santa Caterina del Sasso** (open Easter–Oct: daily 8.30am–noon and 2.30–6pm; Nov–Easter 8.30am–noon and 2–5pm). A 12th-century chapel on the site became a small Dominican monastery, which was spared destruction in the 17th century when a landslide stopped within feet of the church. The site immediately became a place of pilgrimage. However, 270 years later, in 1910, another landslide smashed through the church roof; fortunately, no one was hurt second time around.

The church and the small monastery are at their most impressive when viewed from the lake. Inside, stunning frescoes include the 16th-century *Danse Macabre* in the convent's loggia.

Note that access is by boat from April to September, or by road – but steep steps still need to be negotiated.

LAKE VARESE

With its own little lake, Lago di Varese, nearby, the pleasant town of Varese was founded on the shoe-manufacturing industry (which sadly did not survive to see the 21st century). It is located 56 km (35 miles) northwest of Milan and makes a convenient stop for drivers heading for the Laveno car ferry at Lake Maggiore. Pick up some typical Varese snacks for the ride at the locally famous Panifico Trainini (Via Sacco, 12).

The handsome public gardens, **Giardini Pubblici**, beyond the fine Baroque **Palazzo Estense** that serves as the town hall, offer a great view north to the nearby Alps. Laid out in classical Italian style, the beautiful gardens harbour the 18th-century Villa Mirabello, home to the **Museo Civico** (municipal museum), which is a small museum devoted to local affairs. The museum's collection includes various antiquities unearthed from throughout the surrounding area and a selection of paintings by historic artists from Varese.

Wine Lakes

The fertility of the lake district emerged in the wake of the glaciation that formed the lake basins, and retreated at the end of the Ice Age. One fortuitous effect of the mild climate and myriad micro-climates is the number of vineyards in the region. Asti Spumante is produced in pressure tanks, using a special technique for processing the must of muscat grapes. The full-bodied reds of Barolo and Barbaresco come from the west shore of Lake Maggiore. Both are produced from Nebbiolo grapes, and aged in oak or chestnut casks – Barolo for at least three years, Barbaresco for two. Dry Soave, fruity Valpolicella and dry Bardolino come from around Lake Garda. There are also white wines from Lombardy, including Moscato and Rieslingp; red Valtellina wines from the mountains; and the superior range of Franciacorta wines from Lake Iseo.

LAKE COMO

Embraced by green wooded escarpments, with the Alps soaring impressively above, the Lago di Como (Lake Como) has a certain wistful atmosphere. Its beauty once drew some of England's most romantic 19th-century poets, including Wordsworth, Shelley and Byron, and it continues to attract visitors, whether Italians in search of weekend relaxation or tourists in need of a break from city sightseeing.

The lake's three elongated arms meet at the promontory of its principal resort, Bellagio. The main river feeding the lake is the Adda, flowing in from the north and through the southeast arm at Lecco, the last stronghold of Como's old-fashioned *lucie* fishing boats. Trains from Milan to the town of Como take about an hour, making this a possible day trip.

Como

Known for centuries as a silk-manufacturing centre, Como (population 50,000) lies some 50km (30 miles) up the A9 *autostrada* from Milan. The *centro storico* retains the chequerboard plan of the ancient Roman town of Comum. Also famous for its library and schools, Como was the home of classical writers Pliny the Elder (who died while observing the volcanic eruption of Mt Vesuvius that

Spectacular scenery at Lake Como

engulfed Pompeii on 24 August AD 79) and his nephew and adopted son, Pliny the Younger (AD 62–120).

Como's other famous son, 18th-century electricity pioneer Alessandro Volta, is honoured with a monument in Piazza Volta. The neoclassical **Tempio Volta**, in the lakefront **Giardini Pubblici** (Public Gardens), displays the scientific instruments, namely the battery, with which he developed the 'volt' as a unit of electrical measurement.

The **Lungo Lario** lakefront promenade is the natural setting for the town's *passeggiata* (afternoon stroll), past the cruiseboats' landing stage, and the hotels, cafés and restaurants on **Piazza Cavour**, a popular meeting place in the evenings.

> **From Como, continue along the western bank via Aregno, towards Tremezzo and the village of Mezzegra, where Mussolini was shot dead on 27 April 1945. He and his mistress, Claretta Petacci, were taken to Milan on the day after their execution, and their dead bodies were strung up for all to see in Piazzale Loreto.**

The town's handsome, 15th-century **cathedral** is crowned by a superb Baroque dome added in 1744 by Turin's great architect, Filippo Juvarra. On the façade, both Elder and Younger Pliny are portrayed in seated sculptures on either side of the central doorway. In the lofty Gothic interior, notice the nine 16th-century **tapestries** in the nave, and in the south aisle chapels, altar paintings by Bernardino Luini, in particular *The Holy Conversation*. Next to the cathedral is the arcaded 13th-century **Broletto** (town hall) in white, grey and pink marble.

Most of the shops in town offer fashions for both men and women, as well as accessories from the area's silk mills, still supplying everyone from Valentino's haute couture line to the Vatican with some of the world's finest silk products.

Bellagio

This tranquil resort juts out into the lake on a hilly promontory. Up on the heights above the town, the elegant 18th-century **Villa Serbelloni** (not to be confused with the Villa Serbelloni luxury hotel down near the lakefront) stands in the middle of a beautiful park of rose trees, camellias, magnolias and pomegranates open to the public. At the southern end of town, the lido offers a bracing swim.

Lake cruises and the car ferry leave from the Lungolago Marconi. When looking for gifts, remember that Bellagio craftsmen are also renowned for their silk weaving, as well as olive-wood carving.

Varenna

At the widest part of the lake (4.5km/3 miles) lies **Varenna**, with its picturesque centre of piled-up houses intersected by narrow alleys and dominated by the tower of the parish church of San Giorgio. Varenna makes an excellent base for visiting the lake, as it is the main ferry port. Above the town (345m/1,135ft) is the ruin of the Castello di Vezio, believed to have been built for Queen Theodolinda.

Excursions around Lake Como

Lake Como's most attractive stretch of water is its southwest arm. If you're based at Bellagio, the only way to see the colourful grottoes and misty waterfall at **Nesso** is by taking a boat cruise south from Lezzeno. At **Cernobbio**, just north of Como, the 16th-century Villa d'Este is now one of the world's most fabled hotels *(see page 135)*, where you can 'take tea' and stroll in its manicured grounds.

Varenna's bold architecture

Between the genteel resort towns of **Tremezzo** and **Cadenabbia**, you'll find one of the lake's most beautiful residences (open to the public), the 18th-century **Villa Carlotta**. There's a marvellous view of the lake from its terraced gardens, which are famous for their camellias, azaleas and rhododendrons in late April and May.

Lake Garda's Manerba from the Rocca di Manerba

LAKE GARDA

Surrounded by rolling green hills, Lago di Garda (Lake Garda) is graced with vineyards (notably those of Bardolino), lemon trees, olive groves and cedars. People seeking a restful holiday enjoy its mild winters and mellow summers, and Garda has long been popular with visitors from Austria, Switzerland and Germany. On the west shore, the people of Salò, where Gasparo Bertolotti is said to have designed the violin, suggest his inspiration came from the contours of the lake. Italy's largest lake is shaped less like a violin than a banjo, however, measuring 50km (30 miles) from the cliffs at the tip of its neck down to the base of the broad 'sound box'. At its widest, it stretches 18km (11 miles); its surface is 370 sq km (145 sq miles).

The town of Brescia is the most convenient of the large towns on the way to Garda, with rail and *autostrada* links to the resort town of Desenzano del Garda, some 120 km (75 miles) from Milan.

Gardesana Occidentale (West Shore)

From Salò to Riva alone, a total of 70 tunnels had to be blown out of the rock to build the road along Lake Garda's western shore. Car drivers may be rather confused at all the light and shade, but passengers will glimpse a whole series of superb Mediterranean-style vistas. Even in heavy traffic the route can easily be covered in an hour, not including detours. Visiting only a few of the sights can easily take up a day, however.

First stop is the lively resort of Desenzano del Garda. The attractive, arcaded **Piazza Capelletti** on the lakefront is a lovely place for a drink – or simply to watch the world go by. Next en route is the attractive resort town of **Salò**, set in a narrow bay. With its historical museum contained within the 16th-century Palazzo della Magnifica Patria, it attempts to live down its regrettable moment in history as the capital of Mussolini's puppet republic, which was installed here by the Germans in September 1943.

Continue north to **Gardone Riviera**, a fashionable resort much appreciated for its parks and botanical gardens, and as a base for hikes up and around **Monte Lavino**. Above the town, in Gardone di Sopra, is a 20th-century 'folly', **Il Vittoriale**, the bizarre and disturbing residence of Gabriele d'Annunzio, poet, adventurer and Fascist. Melancholy gardens of dense shrubbery, dark laurel and parades of cypresses lead past a Greek theatre to a mausoleum with the writer's green marble sarcophagus flanked by those of his disciples. It overlooks the prow of a World War I warship, the *Puglia*, which was hauled up the hillside as the *pièce de résistance* of this macabre villa-museum.

The villa houses two cars in which d'Annunzio drove himself to the World War I battlefront and the aircraft from which he dropped his propaganda leaflets over Vienna. His library includes a collection of precious 16th-century books, rare manuscripts and also an Austrian machine gun.

San Zegno di Montagna, a typical Garda mountain village

Gardesana Orientale (East Shore)

The scenic stretch of road known as the Gardesana Orientale was completed in 1926, but today has sadly become one of the most-travelled routes in the region.

The route is varied in geographical terms, leading from Alpine mountains across rolling hills to the broad southern plain, and from the surfing paradises of Riva and Torbole, past the mighty Monte Baldo massif and the gentle Bardolino wine region, to reach the elegant thermal resort of Sirmione at the end of its narrow peninsula. Much of this road can also be covered by bus.

Tradition and elegance are the two most striking characteristics of **Riva**, situated at the northern end of Lake Garda, where the reflections of the steep foothills of the Alps shimmer in the turquoise water. Reminders of the town's Roman origins are still visible in the old walls, while the old town's medieval tangle of little streets are flanked by the spectacular lakeside promenade. Riva has long been a favourite of writers and poets. Goethe called it a 'miracle of nature', and was followed here by Stendhal, Kafka, Thomas Mann and D.H. Lawrence.

Further southeast is **Malcesine**, a former fishing village that now exists almost exclusively from tourism. However, this little place still has much of its ancient charm.

Continuing south takes you to the town of **Garda**, notable for its lovely promenade. Just 3 km (2 miles) further west is the cypress-lined headland of **Punta San Vigilio**. From here, in the Villa Guarnienti's Italian-style gardens, you can enjoy one of the lake's loveliest views. Further along the lakeside road is **Bardolino**, internationally renowned for its lusty red wines. In the town are two picturesque medieval churches, the 9th-century San Zeno and 12th-century San Severo, and the remains of a Scaligeri castle.

At the southeastern tip of the lake is the historic resort town of **Peschiera**, which has retained old ramparts from its late days as a stronghold of the Venetian empire. And at the very south of the lake, perched on a narrow promontory, is the fishing village and spa resort of **Sirmione**. At the tip of the promontory in a romantic setting of olive trees are the **Grotte di Catullo**, the vaulted ruins of a Roman villa. They are often attributed to the ancient poet Catullus, who had his summer residence at Sirmione in the 1st century BC. Fresco fragments from the same period can be seen in the site's **Antiquarium**. One of the best vantage points in town is the tower of the 13th-century castle, **Rocca Scaligera**, built out on to the water beside the town gate by the Scaligeri lords of nearby Verona.

Sirmione's *Stazione Termale* (spa) on the northern edge of town is here to help restore tired bones and muscles, skin problems and breathing, from March to November. The Boiola sulphur springs, famous since ancient Roman times, rise from the lake bed just north of the peninsula at a temperature of 69°C (156°F).

WHAT TO DO

There are plenty of things to do other than sightseeing in and around Milan and the lakes. We offer some suggestions here for shopping, entertainment, sports and what to do with the kids.

SHOPPING

Milan and the lake resorts are full of great buys, but don't expect to find too many bargains. The Milanese know the full value of their design sense and tend to put an appropriate price on it.

What to Buy

Antiques: The Via Montenapoleone and Brera districts *(see pages 45 and 42, respectively)* are the heart of the antiques dealers' territory. Of the many interesting and respectable choices, try: L'Oro dei Farlocchi at 5 Via Madonnina for Italian **Medieval and Baroque furniture**; on 22 Via Spiga, visit Subert for **scientific instruments**; and, at 46 Via Spiga, Brucoli offers a selection of beautiful antique **jewellery**.

Clothes: Milan is Italy's undisputed fashion capital, and the centuries-old Italian sense of style and colour quite often is the source of inspiration for designs seen in Paris, New York and Tokyo. Some designer clothes may be cheaper back home, but you will find a much greater selection here, and the latest styles are aften shown in Milanese stores first. For both women's and men's clothes, the master couturiers Versace, Prada, Armani, Moschino, Missoni, Fendi, Gucci, Ermenegildo Zegna and Gianfranco Ferré all have their boutiques on and around the celebrated 'Montenapo',

Homegrown fashion: Prada Milan

Stylish Milanese footwear

principally along Via Montenapoleone itself and its off-shoots such as Via della Spiga and Via Sant'Andrea.

For the very best in Italian **shoes,** try Cesare Paciotti, Ferragamo, Bruno Magli and Fratelli Rossetti; for **lingerie**, Pratesi or La Perla; for exclusive **beachwear,** Cavallini; for the softest, most exquisitely fashioned **leather** visit Gucci, Bottega Veneto and Nazareno Gabrielli.

Children's fashion can be found around the city at Prenatal. **Fiorucci,** situated in the Gallery Passarella at San Babila, is a Milanese icon, selling all the latest high fashion casual wear, household gadgets and other fun accessories for the discerning young customer.

There is also the possibility of buying **second-hand** high fashion from Mercatino Michela, with five locations (tel: 02-799748 for addresses) in the form of 'sample sales'. Diehard bargain hunters should take time to seek out special **outlets** in Milan and its suburbs. Ask the tourist information office *(see page 128)* for a full listing.

Cosmetics: You can find **handmade cosmetics,** soaps and fragrances at Lusc at 6 Via Fiori Chiari in the Brera. Another source of natural and creative **hair- and bodycare products** is an *erborista*, such as the Centro Erboristico Milanese, at 3 Via Melzo.

Craftwork: The quality of traditional craftsmanship outside Milan can still be admired in the ornaments and utensils of wrought iron, turned wood and embossed copper on sale in the pretty city of Bergamo. Lake Maggiore resorts are especially known for Arona ceramics, Como and Bellagio for silk and carved olive wood, and Brescia for hunting rifles.

Gourmet Foods: In Milan, the great gift speciality is the gargantuan *panettone* – a sweet, egg-based holiday loaf with raisins. You will find it most commonly displayed in any fine *pasticceria* before and during the Christmas season. There are many small delicatessens all over the city and the resort areas carrying local specialities. You will find the largest selection of producers for regional products sold in their native area; for example if you plan to visit Lake Garda, wait to make your olive oil purchase there. For a full array of other Lombardy specialities visit the famous **Peck**, Via Speronari 3 (Metro: Duomo), which has just combined all of their little shops into one large, two-storey centre. Go

Milanese Markets

There are around a dozen street markets in Milan set up from 8.30am to 1pm each day, selling everything from fruit to footwear to kitchen gadgets. Every Saturday from 8.30am to 5pm, one of the largest, the Fiera di Senigallia, is held on Viale G. D'Annunzio, along the Darsena Basin, with a wide assortment of wares. The most popular antiques market takes place on nearby Via Ripa Porta Ticinese, along the Naviglio Grande on the last Sunday of each month (except July). Vendors set up at dawn and tend to close after lunch. Rather more chic (and expensive) is the antiques market held in the Brera neighbourhood on the third Saturday of each month, along Via Fiori Chiari, Via Madonnina and Piazza Formentini. It starts a little later (10am), but some stalls stay open well past dusk.

Erboristas **sell attractive bath and beauty products**

upstairs and grab a table to sit and enjoy the delicacies that have caught your eye.

Household Accessories: Milan has an unrivalled range of innovative styles in everything from fountain pens and lamps to kitchenware, espresso machines and other household gadgets. The best-known household gadget designer is **Alessi**, with its own store at 9 Corso Matteotti. More serious Italian kitchenware afficionados should visit the **Medagliani** warehouse store in the small mall at Via San Gregorio 43. **G. Lorenzi** in Via Montenapoleone 9 carries a fine selection of knives and other tableware.

Jewellery: The country's top jewellers share the 'Montenapo' district with the fashion designers. The leading shops are: Bulgari, Buccellati, Calderoni, Jacente and Dal Vecchio (for antique jewellery).

Lake Garda's goldsmiths are highly respected, with boutiques at all the major resorts, and Brescia is known for its fine silverware. For upmarket designer watches, many take the cruise on Lake Maggiore across the Swiss frontier to Locarno, where you'll find the greatest selection. Otherwise, try **Centro P. R. Lorenz** at Via Montenapoleone 12, in central Milan.

Modern Furniture: Even if you're not contemplating carrying an armchair home, it can be interesting to do some astute window shopping in Milan to help place early orders with distributors back where you live. The major stores of international fame are conveniently grouped along Via Manzoni. For the hottest new kitchens the Boffi showroom is on the nearby Via Solferino 11.

Textiles: Como and its environs have been renowned as a silk-producing hub for centuries, and its looms continue to produce the highest-quality silks, used for fashion, accessories and home furnishings for top-drawer clients as diverse as designer fashion house Prada and the Pope. In Como, the retail outlet of the world-famous Ratti factory, based at Via Cernobbi 17, on the road to the Villa d'Este Hotel, offers a wide selection of silks.

Toys: Long before Geppetto made Pinocchio, Italian toys, especially puppets, were widely renowned. For the delight of children, visit a few of the best Milan toy shops, namely: Cagnoni, Corso Vercelli 38 (Metro: Conciliazione); Giocattoli e Giochi, Città del Sole, Via Orefici 5 (Metro: Cairoli); and Toys Center, Via Mauro Macchi 29 (situated near Stazione Centrale).

ENTERTAINMENT

During the extensive renovation of La Scala *(see page 33)*, **opera** is being performed at the **Teatro degli Arcimboldi**, in zona Bicocca northwest of the station. Information on the current season and tickets is available on La Scala's website <www.teatroallascala.org>; also tel: 02-860775 for bookings.

Traditionally, Milan's opera season opens with a gala pre-
mière on St Ambrose's feast day, on December 7 – if you are
offered a ticket for this occasion, jump at the chance. Ballet
is also performed at the Teatro degli Arcimboldi throughout
the season.

Classical music concerts are much in demand in cultural
Milan, most notably at the Teatro Filodrammatici, e-mail
<filodrammatici@tiscilinet.it> , located near La Scala, on Via
Filodrammatici; and at the Auditorium di Milano Orchestra
Sinfonica G. Verdi, <www.orchestrasinfonica.milano.it>, on
Via Torricelli. **Ballet** is also staged at the Teatro Nazionale,
<www.teatronazionale.com>, Piazza Piemonte 12.

Open-air concerts are regularly held in summer in Milan,
at the Castello Sforzesco's Piazza d'Armi, as well as
in the various lake resorts. Bergamo's delightful Teatro
Donizetti makes an attractive venue for excellent-quality

The lavish interior of La Scala

opera, ballet and classical music performances.

Even if your Italian is not up to scratch, for **theatre** it may still be worth your while attending one of the lively productions presented at the world-renowned Piccolo Teatro–Teatro Grassi; <www.piccoloteatro.org>; Via Rovello 2, created by the great Giorgio Strehler. The troupe's communicative style should transcend any language problems.

For film buffs, there are over 100 cinemas across Milan, with most of the big screens grouped around Corso Vittorio Emanuele II. The majority of films shown in Milan are dubbed.

On the west side of town, the Palalido and Palazzetto dello Sport present large-scale **jazz** and **rock music** concerts. Palatrussardi, on Via S. Elia, also stages a variety of major musical events.

You can enjoy music in a more intimate setting, over a drink, at the bars in the Navigli (canal) quarters, to the southwest of the city. This area really comes into its own at night, when the multitude of bars and restaurants alongside Milan's network of canals offer extensive drinking and dining options. Or, do as the Milanese do and take a civilised evening promenade *(passeggiata)* along here.

The Tunnel on Via Sammartini 30 behind Stazione Centrale has live music on the weekends with a DJ afterwards. If you are looking for a pub-type atmosphere (Italian style), try Bar Magenta at the corner of Corso Magenta and Via Carducci (Metro: Cadorna), which offers an abundant spread during the aperitif hour, and sandwiches and snacks throughout the night.

Stop off at Caffe' della Pusterla on Via de Amicis 24, where the bartender will entertain you while preparing a cocktail, then head off to one of Milan's many **clubs** such as Hollywood or Shocking, both near Stazione Garibaldi.

SPORTS

As in all Italian cities, football (soccer) rules in Milan, but there are plenty of other sporting activities offered as well. For more detailed information about access to Milan's sporting facilities, contact Milanosport, Piazza Diaz 1A; tel: 02-801466, fax: 02-801460.

Participant Sports

Tennis and Golf: The most easily accessible tennis courts (covered and open, hard and clay) from the city centre are at the Lido di Milano, Piazzale Lotto 15 (Metro: Lotto); tel: 02-39266100. Golf Club Milano's 9- and 18-hole courses are located in Monza's Villa Reale Park, entrance at Porta San Giorgio; tel: 039-303081. Check with the Milan tourist information office about temporary membership.

Baseball and Basketball: Appropriate to its name, the Centro Sportivo Kennedy, Via Olivieri 15, tel: 02-47996783, has a very respectable baseball diamond, while the Lido di Milano has a good basketball court.

Swimming and Watersports: The Lido di Milano also has a heated indoor pool (as well as a **gymnasium** for a pre-swimming workout). A little further out at the Parco Forlanini on the east side of town, the Saini sports centre, Via Corelli 136, has the above plus an open-air pool.

Swimming in the lakes can be a very bracing affair, but the major resorts do offer amenities for **water-skiing**, **windsurfing** and **sailing**. For details of **fishing** in the lakes, enquire at local tourist information offices.

Spectator Sports

There can be few more exciting sporting spectacles in Europe than a **football** (soccer) match out at the Meazza Stadium (San Siro), Via Piccolomini 5. The city's two teams, AC Milan and

Inter, are among the best in the world. All their games involve high drama, but when the two teams play against each other, all eyes are on the field.

There is also **horse-racing** at the San Siro race course, while **ice-hockey** matches take place at the Palazzo del Ghiaccio, Via Piranesi 14 (Stazione Porta Vittoria).

Motor rallies are held during the summer around Bergamo, Brescia and Como. The biggest sporting event in the region is still the **Grand Prix** Formula 1 motor race, which is held at Monza in September.

Windsurfing on Lake Garda

MILAN WITH CHILDREN

The secret to keeping children amused in Milan is to make the most of the city's sights, even if they're not geared - specifically towards kids. At the **Duomo** *(see page 27)* for instance, a visit to the cathedral roof is always a great success. Also popular are Leonardo da Vinci's inventions at the **Science Museum** *(see page 50)*. Taking to the water is usually a successful ploy: in Milan itself there are **canal cruises** on the Navigli *(see page 56)*, although more interesting are countless boat trips up and down the shores of the Lombard lakes. Youngsters may also enjoy the sports museum located at the stadium at San Siro (tel: 02-4042432).

Parks: Milan has two very large parks in close proximity to the city centre. Behind the Castello Sforzesco. **Parco Sempione** (Metro: Lanza) provides lots of space for the kids to run around and let off steam. Besides its tropical fish, the **aquarium** (Via Gadio 2) has a wonderful collection of reptiles. In August, the park hosts a summer festival, *Vacanze a Milano* (Holidays in Milan), offering free theatre and musical shows, dancing and open-air restaurants.

In the **Giardini Pubblici** (Metro: Palestro), you will find duck ponds, pony-rides, bumper cars and a miniature train. There is also a **Planetarium** here and dinosaurs in the **Natural History Museum**.

Puppets: Not far from the Science Museum is the Teatro delle Marionette, a privately run puppet theatre at Via Olivetani 3B; tel: 02-4694440 (Metro: Conciliazione). When visiting the Borromean Islands on Lake Maggiore *(see page 71)*, visit the 18th-century puppets in the *palazzo* on Isola Bella. And you can always head for Milan's toyshops *(see page 89)*.

Special Events: Every Saturday morning **stamp** and **coin collectors** exchange treasures on the Piazza degli Affari by the *Borso* (Metro: Cordusio). You will find bargain buys within pocket-money range. A plant and small animal market is held on Sunday morning in front of the Palazzo Reale (Mar–Jun and Sep–Dec).

The Giardini Pubblici

In the spring, kids may want to take their dads to the **Monza Motorcycle Grand Prix**. Call the Monza Autodromo; tel: 039-2482212 or visit <www.monzanet.it> for more information, including dates and times.

Calendar of Events

Details of trade and fashion shows in Milan are available from Ente Fiera Milano, Largo Domodossola 1, 20145 Milano; tel: 02-49977908; fax: 02-48193029; <www.fieramilano.com>.

January: Milan. 6 January, Corteo dei Rei Magi (Twelfth Night) procession between Sant'Ambrogio and Sant'Eustorgio.

February: Sei Giorni di Ciclismo (Six Days of Cycling) at forum di Assago; tel: 02-488571; <www.filaforum.it>.

February/March: All cities. Carnival. Street parade, parties.

March: Milan. Via Crema; also Piacenza. 13 March Tredesin de Marz Flower festival marking the day children get their winter hair cut. Antique Book Exhibition International Trade Fair.

April: Bruzzano. Palio della Suca, small horse race in traditional Renaissance costumes.

May: Legnano. Last Sunday. Medieval-style battle and pageant commemorating the 1176 Lombard victory. Brescia: 1000 Miglia vintage car rally.

May–June: Bergamo and Brescia. International piano festival.

June: Milan. Navigli canal district festival; Comacina. Fireworks over Lake Como for midsummer Island Feast of San Giovanni.

July: Besana Brianza. First Sunday. Festa di S. Camillo celebrated at a Visconti villa with music and fireworks in the evening.

August: Milan. Vacanze a Milano festival in Parco Sempione; Gardone. Sailing regatta on Lake Garda.

August–September: Stresa. Settimane Musicale, music festival in churches and on Isola Bella.

September: Monza. Grand Prix Formula I motor racing; Como. Autunno Musicale international music festival (until November); Pavia. Mostro Autunno Pavese, gastronomic festival.

October: Milan. Last Sunday. Sagra del Tartufo, Via Ripamonti, festival centered around truffles.

November: All cities. November 1, All Saints' Day, remembrance with flowers and *pane dei morti* (bread for the dead).

December: Milan. 7 December. Feast day of St Ambrose.

EATING OUT

Until recently the popular view of Italian cuisine was based solely upon Neapolitan, Sicilian and Calabrese dishes, since most Italian immigrants came from these regions. Lighter, more delicate northern cuisine has more recently made its way to our tables. It's usually tasty, simple, colourful and offered in multiple courses, including classics such as *risotto alla Milanese* and the famous *osso buco (see page 98).*

WHERE TO EAT

Most major hotels in Milan and the Lakes offer English- or American-style breakfast buffets, often included in the room rate. If you prefer to breakfast Italian-style, head for a little bar for your *prima colazione.* This is the time to order *cappuccino* sprinkled with powdered cocoa (upon request) to accompany your choice of a *brioche,* ordered *vuoto* (empty), *con la marmalata* (with marmalade) or *la crema* (pastry cream). When ordering tea, you will be asked *al limone o latte* (with lemon or milk). The thick pudding-like *cioccolata calda* (hot chocolate) is almost a meal in itself.

Milan is the home of the *paninoteca* or sandwich bar. Due to the typically fast-paced lifestyle of the hard-working Milanese, there is

> Pavia is famed for its hearty soups *(minestre),* of which the most celebrated is *zuppa pavese,* a broth with egg on toast floating on the top (the egg cooks slowly in the broth). This dish was reportedly served to François I (King of France and of Pavia at that time), to fortify him for the Battle of Pavia in 1525. Although the French lost the battle to the Spanish, the soup is still going strong.

little time for a three-hour Roman-style lunch here. Panino Giusto has several locations around the centre offering more sizeable grilled and cold sandwiches than those offered in most bars. If you want a *primo* (first course) of pasta or risotto, or a salad, stop in a stand-up bar or a *tavola calda* where you can have a quick bite at the counter. Supplies for a picnic in the park or out in the country can be found at a *pizzicheria* (delicatessen).

For dinner, even if you're not overly budget conscious, bear in mind that the most elaborate *ristorante*, where prices match the opulence of the décor, rarely offers the best value. In a relaxed *osteria*, a family-run *trattoria* or a Neapolitan-style *pizzeria*, which will serve much more than simply pizza, both the ambience and the food can be just as enjoyable as a smart *ristorante,* and your evening will generally have more character. In all cases, cover *(coperto)*

Cocktails al fresco

and service *(servizio)* charges are usually included (even then, it's normal to leave something extra); if service is not included, leave about 10–15 percent for the waiter. Reservations are always recommended due to the unpredictable deluge of out-of-town diners in Milan for the frequent trade fairs. Sundays can also be tricky, as much of Milan (and most of its restaurants) closes down on that day.

For more details, see the list of Recommended Restaurants starting on page 137.

WHAT TO EAT

Milan's ethnically mixed population makes for a wide variety of international cuisine. Throughout Lombardy, you'll find not only local specialities but those of other Italian regions as well. A fine selection of vegetarian restaurants have sprung up to satisfy the substantial increase in Italian vegetarians recently. But if you desire the true native experience, stick to local specialities such as risotto, polenta and *osso buco* (stewed veal shank).

Antipasti

The average *trattoria* sets out a colourful display of its *antipasti* (appetisers) near the entrance to tantalise passers-by. Get to know the delicacies on offer by creating your own assortment *(antipasto misto)*. Attractive and tasty are room-temperature *peperoni* – green, yellow and red peppers grilled, skinned and marinated in olive oil and a little lemon juice. Grilled mushrooms *(funghi)*, small courgettes *(zucchini)* and aubergine or eggplant *(melanzane)* are served room-temperature, and artichokes *(carciofi)* and sliced fennel *(finocchio)* are also served raw, with a tangy dressing *(pinzimonio)*. One refreshing hors d'œuvre is the Neapolitan *mozzarella alla caprese*, slices of soft buffalo cheese and tomato with basil, olive oil and black pepper.

Try Sicilian tuna *(tonno)* with white beans and onions *(fagioli e cipolle)*. Mixed seafood appetisers *(antipasto di mare)* may well include: scampi, prawns *(gamberi)*, mussels *(cozze)*, fresh sardines *(sarde)*, squid *(calamari)* and octopus *(polpi)*.

Paper-thin ham from Parma or San Daniele is served with seasonal melon *(prosciutto con melone)* or fresh figs *(con fichi)* when in season. Most salami is mass-produced in Milan factories, but some restaurants do 'import' farm-produced sausage from Emilia-Romagna, Tuscany or Liguria.

Spicy salami

Primi (First Courses)

Although we are used to making a whole meal from a heap of pasta, a more moderate portion here is considered a first dish, or *primo*, to be followed by a *secondo* (main course). The staff generally will not be offended though if you order a *primo* along with an appetiser and dessert.

The most popular soups are mixed vegetable *(mine-strone)*. If you're feeling adventurous, go local and try *ris e ran,* a soup with rice and frogs' legs. Brescia is famous for its soups with tortellini or rice, the latter much more savoury than its name *minestra sporca* or 'dirty soup'.

You'll usually come across the same few dozen variations, but it is said that there are as many different shapes of Italian

Italian staple

pasta as there are Italian dialects, some 360 at the last count, with new forms always being created. Each different sauce – from tomato to cheese, cream, meat or fish – is destined to a specific shape. In this land of artists, the pasta's shape and texture form an essential part of the taste, and pasta manufacturers commission noted designers to create new configurations. Besides spaghetti and macaroni, the wide popularity of pasta has familiarised us with *tagliatelle* (ribbon noodles), *lasagne* (layers of pasta laced with a meat and béchamel sauce), rolled *canelloni* and *ravioli*. From there, you launch into the lusty poetry of *tortellini* and *fagotti* (variations on ravioli), or fat 'tongues' of *linguine*, flat *pappardelle*, quill-shaped *penne* and the corrugated *rigatoni*. None will disappoint: try a different one at each meal.

Following the pasta profusion, there are almost as many **sauces**. A subtle variation on the ubiquitous tomato-based *bolognese* meat sauce is made with chopped chicken livers, white wine and celery. Others range from the simplest and spiciest *aglio, olio, pepperoncino* (garlic, olive oil and hot peppers), *marinara* (tomato with oregano), *carbonara* (chopped bacon and eggs), *pesto* (basil and garlic ground up in olive oil with pine nuts and Parmesan cheese) and *vongole* (clams, sometimes with tomato), to the succulent *lepre* (hare in red wine) and the startling but wonderful *al nero* (pasta blackened by the ink of the cuttlefish). Parmesan is not automatically added to every pasta dish, and sauces using fish and mushroom are meant to be eaten without, so as not to overpower the delicate flavours. Follow your waiter's suggestion.

For Lombardy's princes and peasants alike, the Po Valley paddies have made **risotto** a worthy rival to pasta. The rice has to be round and creamy, never long and dry. Northern tradition cooks it slowly in white wine, beef marrow, butter (not oil) and saffron, with Parmesan cheese melted in at the end of the cooking for the proper smooth finish. Delicious variations result when blended with seafood, chicken, mushrooms or whatever the daily market offers.

Secondi (Main Courses)

Veal *(vitello)* is Lombardy's main meat dish. The popular *cotoletta alla Milanese* (pounded veal cutlet) is known in some restaurants as the 'elephant's ear', as they have pounded it so thin and wide. Brushed with egg, coated with bread-

Risotto alla Milanese

The recipe below, for this ultimate Milanese dish, is true to the original and serves four people. First, soak 20g (½ oz) dried mushrooms in lukewarm water. Next, finely chop a small onion and fry it gently in 30g (1 oz) of butter. Add either 30g (1 oz) of beef marrow or 2 teaspoons of dripping – beef marrow is more traditional – and stir well. Now, take 8 or 9 handfuls of rice and add them to the frying onions; stir well and cook the rice briefly, so that it glistens. Add the rehydrated mushrooms and, gradually, 1 litre (2 pints) of stock. When the rice is cooked, add a pinch of saffron to colour the dish, stir in a generous portion of grated Parmesan and a little more butter, mix well and serve.

crumbs, and pan-fried in butter, it is not exactly a dietary dish, but when in Rome (or Milan)... For something a bit lighter, try *osso buco* (stewed veal shank), the *vitello tonnato* (veal in tuna sauce) or *alla fiorentina* (with spinach sauce).

The Roman *saltimbocca* (literally: 'jump in the mouth') is also a favourite on Lombardian menus, with its veal rolled with ham and sage and cooked in Marsala wine. Calf's liver *(fegato)* is served *alla milanese* in breadcrumbs. Alternatively, it can be served *alla veneziana*, thinly sliced and sautéed with onions in olive oil.

Beef *(manzo)*, lamb *(agnello)*, pork *(maiale)* and chicken *(pollo)* are most often grilled or roasted *(al forno)*. Curious palates might like to tackle Milanese *busecca*, tripe with white beans, or *casoeula*, pork and sausages stewed in cabbage.

Although Milan is not a coastal city it does have a large **fish** market behind the Stazione Centrale. The best seafood

For those with more traditional tastes…

meals are had, though, at restaurants that source directly from the nearby Ligurian shores and the freshwater lakes. Whole fish are prepared simply grilled, steamed, baked under a sea-salt crust or fried. Try the *spigola* (sea bass), *coda di rospa* (angler fish), *triglia* (red mullet) or even *pesce spada* (swordfish). *Fritto misto* usually means a mixed fry of fish, but can also include anything from chicken, calf's liver, veal and vegetables. If in doubt as to what you might be ordering, clarify with your waiter.

Cheeses and Dessert

Grana padana is similar to Parmesan *(parmigiano)*, though the former is indigenous to this region. Besides grated over a *primo*, it is eaten by itself, and delicious with a drizzle of *aceto balsamico tradizionale* (balsamic vinegar). Try, too, the creamy blue *gorgonzola* from the nearby town of the same name, aromatic *bagoss* or a creamy chunk of aged *robiola*.

During the Easter and Christmas holidays look for the famous Milanese *colomba* or *panettone*, both egg-based leavened sweet breads studded with raisins. In some restaurants you will find local *torta di tagliatelle*, a dessert made from egg, almonds and cocoa. A more neutral finish to your meal is the Mantovan cornmeal-based *torta sbrisolona*.

Seasonal **fruit** is a lighter way to end the meal: grapes *(uva)*, apples *(mele)* and tart blood oranges *(torchi)* in the autumn and winter; apricots *(albicocche)*, peaches *(pesche)* and wonderful fresh figs *(fichi)* in spring and summer.

Ice-cream comes in a variety of flavours and is generally best when bought from an ice-cream parlour *(gelateria)*.

DRINKS

The wines from Lake Garda's east shores falling under the DOC zone of *Riviera del Garda* include *rosso* (red) and *chiaretto* (rosé). Other reds from the DOC zone of Oltrepò Pavese include

Local red wines

Barbacarlo, *Barbera* and *Rosso*. The *Francacorta* DOC from the Brescia area includes reds, sparkling and still whites, as well as rosé.

You may also venture into the products of other regions such as Piedmont's splendid, full-bodied *Barolo*, a young Tuscan *Chianti Classico*, which is distinguished by the proud *gallo nero* (black rooster), a complex *Brunello* from further south in Tuscany, or a dry white *Orvieto* from Umbria.

To help you digest your meal, try a *digestivo* of sweet *limoncello* from the south, a strong, clear *grappa* or an *amaro*, literally translated as 'bitter'.

To Help You Order ...

What do you recommend?	**Cosa consiglia?**
Do you have a set menu?	**Avete un menù a prezzo fisso?**
I'd like a/an/some...	**Vorrei...**

black pepper	**peperoni**	salt	**sale**
butter	**burro**	sugar	**zucchero**
bread	**pane**	water	**acqua**

... and Read the Menu

aglio	garlic	**birra**	beer
agnello	lamb	**bistecca**	beef steak
arancia	orange	**caffè**	coffee

carciofi	artichokes	**ostrica**	oyster
carne	meat	**pancetta**	bacon
cipolle	onions	**patate**	potatoes
coniglio	rabbit	**pepe**	peppers
costoletta	cutlet	**pesca**	peach
cozze	mussels	**pesce**	fish
crostacei	shellfish	**piselli**	peas
fichi	figs	**pollo**	chicken
formaggio	cheese	**pomodoro**	tomato
frutta	fruit	**tè**	tea
gamberi	scampi, prawns	**uova**	egg
		verdura	greens
gelato	ice cream	**vino**	wine
insalata	salad	**bianco**	white
latte	milk	**rosato**	rosé
mela	apple	**rosso**	red
minestra	soup	**vitello**	veal

Toni's Bread

Many great things were born of a mistake. The now-famous Milanese panettone was a quick recovery from a dessert gone wrong. Legend goes that it was Christmas Eve at the Castello Sforzesco under the reign of Ludovico, and the grand banquet was to finish with the court chef's secret-recipe dessert. After perhaps one *grappa* too many, the chef lost track of time and burned his creation. While he was fretting and desperate, Toni the dishwasher took the leftover dough of the original dessert, added candied fruit, spices, eggs and sugar and popped it in the oven. When he took it out, it looked like a simple loaf of bread, but there was no alternative to offer. Dressed up on a silver tray and served in great style, it elicited perplexed reactions, but the final result was a success. Toni's bread (pane di toni) has evolved into today's plump panettone traditionally served during the Christmas season.

HANDY TRAVEL TIPS

An A–Z Summary of Practical Information

A

ACCOMMODATION *(alloggio; see also page 130)*

Hotels. Called *hotels or alberghi*, hotels are classified in categories ranging from five stars (luxury) down to one. Rates vary according to location, season, class and services, and are fixed in agreement with the regional tourist boards in Milan and the lakes. Being an important business city, Milan's high- and low-season rates for hotels are determined mainly by frequent trade fairs and other commercial considerations outside the summer months, with several hotels in Milan even closing in August. At the lake resorts, where many hotels close after Christmas (or even before that, November to Easter), low season varies but usually runs from May through June and late-September to October.

Breakfast is usually included, but even if prices are listed as *tutto compreso* (inclusive of local taxes and service charges), check that the VAT sales tax (IVA) of 20 percent for five-star hotels and 10% for other categories is included.

I'd like a single/double room.	**Vorrei una camera singola/matromoniale.**
with bath/shower/private toilet	**con bagno/doccia/ gabinetto privato**
What's the rate per night/week?	**Qual è il prezzo per una notte/una settimana?**

It is advisable year round and essential in high season to book reservations in advance through travel agencies or by contacting the hotel directly; always get written confirmation. Once there, the tourist information offices *(see page 128)* can supply local hotel lists. At Milan's Linate and Malpensa airports and the Stazione Centrale train station, information desks provide advice and booking facilities.

Pensione. This term covers everything from a small, family-run hotel (with breakfast included) to an elegant inn of a higher category. Those with shared bathrooms are rare, but they do still exist.

Self-catering accommodation. Families staying for a week or longer in one place may find it convenient and economical, especially in tourist resorts, to rent a furnished apartment or villa.

   For further information contact: <www.italianvillas.com> or Agriturist, the National Association for Rural Tourism: Corso Vittorio Emanuele 101, 00186 Rome; tel: 06-6852342; fax: 06-6852424; <www.agriturist.it>.

AIRPORTS *(aeroporti)*

Milan has two airports, **Malpensa**, located 45 km (28 miles) northwest of the city centre, and used for intercontinental traffic, and **Linate**, situated about 7 km (4 miles) to the east and used mainly for domestic and European flights. There is a bus service (tel: 02-6690351) to Milan's central railway station, Stazione Centrale, approximately every 30 minutes, 6.05am–11.35pm from Linate and every 20 minutes, 4.15am–12.15am from Malpensa.
Malpensa and Linate Airport information: tel: 02-7485220; <www.sea-aeroportmilano.it/Eng>. Lost baggage: Malpensa tel: 02-58580069; Linate tel: 02-70124451.

Could you please take these bags to the bus/train/taxi	**Mi porti queste valige fino all'autobus/al treno/al taxi, per favore**
What time does the train/bus leave for the city centre?	**A che ora parte il treno/pullman per il centro?**

Bergamo has an airport at Orio (for domestic flights), around 45 km (28 miles) from Milan; tel: 035-326323.

B

BUDGETING FOR YOUR TRIP

Milan, a business-expense town, is fairly expensive in line with other major European cities. The following prices are for guidance only.

Airport bus. To central Milan from Linate: €0.75–2.50, depending on the service; from Malpensa around €7.

Camping. €6 per person per night (children €2); car, caravan (trailer or camper) €8–12 per night; tent €6 per night; motorcycle free.

Car hire/rental. Booked on arrival in Milan, with unlimited mileage but collision/theft insurance and 20 percent tax extra: medium-range (Fiat Tipo) €120 per day, €550 per week.

Entertainment. Cinema €7; club (entrance and first drink) €10–20; opera €12–120.

Hotels. Double occupancy with private bathrooms per night, including service and taxes, no meals: inexpensive €50–85, moderate €85–180, luxury €180–600. *(See also page 130.)*

Meals and drinks. Continental breakfast €2–15; lunch or dinner in a good restaurant (including service but not wine) €20–40; bottle of wine, from €3; beer/soft drinks €1.50–4; aperitif €2.50–4; coffee served at a table €1.75–3.50, at the bar €0.75–2.

Museums. €1–8.

Public transport. Metro/bus/tram tickets €1 each; day-travel pass €3, two-day pass €5.50.

Taxis. Central Milan to Linate airport approximately €15–17.50; to Malpensa airport around €9; average trip in Milan €6–10.

Youth hostels. €13–15 per night, with breakfast.

C

CAMPING *(campeggio)*

You'll find plenty of campsites around the lakes and in the Milan area, notably the one at **Città di Milano**, Via Gaetano Airaghi, 61 (near Tangenziale Ovest motorway); tel: 02-48200134; fax: 02-48202999; call in advance to confirm dates. Alternatively, another Milan site is out at the **Autodromo di Monza**, Località Biassono; tel: 039-387771; fax: 039-320324; open April to September. Addresses and details of amenities for the Lombardy region are given in the directory *Campeggi in Italia*, published by the Italian Touring Club (TCI), Corso Italia 10, 20122 Milan, tel: 02-8526304 or 02-5359971; <www.touringclub.it/english>. A free list of sites with location map, published by the Federcampeggio *(Federazione Italiana del Campeggio e del Caravanning)*, is available from the Italian National Tourist Office *(see page 128)* or from Federcampeggio: Via Vittorio Emanuele 11, 50041 Calenzano (Florence); tel: 055-882 391.

Campsites at the lakes are usually very crowded during the peak summer months of July and August. Check with local tourist offices *(see page 128)* for information about reservations. Many campsites require guests to carry the *International Camping Carnet*, a pass that entitles holders to discounts and insurance coverage throughout Europe. The Carnet can be obtained through your camping or automobile association or from the TCI or Federcampeggio.

Is there a campsite near here?	**C'è un campeggio qui vicino?**
Have you room for a tent/ caravan?	**C'è posto per una tenda/ roulotte?**
May we camp here?	**Possiamo campeggiare qui?**

CAR HIRE/RENTAL *(autonoleggio; see also page 113)*

Driving in Milan is taxing and not recommended to the uninitiated, so do all your sightseeing in the city, then rent a car for out-of-town excursions or to proceed to your next stop.

The best rates are usually found by booking directly with an international rental company and paying for your car before you leave home, or as part of a 'fly-drive' package. Check that the quoted rate includes Collision Damage Waiver, unlimited mileage and tax, and whether the car has to be returned to its starting point (eg clarify an airport vs central location, as they may result in different rates), as these can greatly increase the cost.

You will need a driver's licence (EU model for EU citizens) for at least 12 months, shown at the time of rental. You will also need to show your passport and a major credit card. Minimum age is 21 or 25 depending on the company and the car's engine size. Fuel *(benzina)* is priced per litre (4 litres per gallon) and can cost about €1/litre.

CLIMATE *(clima)*

In the Po Valley, summers are very hot and humid, while winters are cold and foggy. Temperatures are at their most extreme in and directly around Milan itself; the lake regions are generally a couple of degrees cooler. The best time to visit Milan is in spring or autumn between April and June or in September. As the luxuriant vegetation testifies, winters around the lakes can offer surprisingly mild days, but can also be as bitingly cold. The chart below shows the maximum average temperature, per month.

	J	F	M	A	M	J	J	A	S	O	N	D
°C	5	8	13	18	23	27	29	29	24	17	10	6
°F	40	46	56	65	74	80	84	85	75	63	51	43

COMPLAINTS

To avoid problems, always establish prices in advance, such as when dealing with porters at stations. For complaints about taxi fares, refer to a notice, in four languages, affixed by law in each taxi, specifying extra charges (airport runs, Sunday or holiday rates, night or baggage surcharge) in excess of the meter rate.

CRIME AND SAFETY

Cases of violence against tourists are rare, but petty theft is a problem, especially pickpockets in busy markets and on buses. Beware of gypsy girls with babies or young children – while they distract your attention begging for coins, an accomplice may be behind you dipping into pockets and bags. Don't carry large amounts of cash and leave your valuables in the hotel safe, not in your room. Make photocopies of your tickets, driving licence, passport and other vital documents to facilitate reporting a theft and obtaining replacements.

Any theft or loss must be reported immediately to the police and you should obtain a copy of the report in order to comply with your travel insurance. If your passport is lost or stolen, you should also inform your consulate or embassy *(see page 116)*.

I want to report a theft.	**Voglio denunciare un furto.**
My wallet/passport/ticket has been stolen.	**Mi hanno rubato il portafoglio/ il passaporto/il biglietto.**

CUSTOMS AND ENTRY REQUIREMENTS

For citizens of EU countries, a valid passport or identity card is all that is needed to enter Italy for up to 90 days. Citizens of Australia, New Zealand and the US also need only a valid passport.

Visas. For stays of more than 90 days a visa *(permesso di soggiorno)* or residence permit is required. For full information on passport and visa regulations check with the Italian Embassy in your country *(see page 116)*.

Customs. Free exchange of non-duty-free goods – for personal use only – is allowed between EU countries. Refer to your home country's regulating organisation for a current and complete list of import restrictions.

Currency restrictions. Tourists may bring an unlimited amount of Italian or foreign currency into the country. On departure, however, you must declare any currency beyond the equivalent of €10,000, so it's wise to declare sums exceeding this amount when you arrive.

I've nothing to declare.	**Non ho niente da dichiarare.**
It's for my personal use.	**È per mio uso personale.**

D

DRIVING

Motorists planning to take their vehicle into Italy need a full driver's licence accompanied by a translation (available from your local automobile association), an International Motor Insurance Certificate and a Vehicle Registration Document. Drivers entering Italy in a private car registered to another person must have the owner's written permission, translated. A green insurance card is not a legal requirement, but it is strongly recommended for travel within Italy. Foreign visitors must display an official nationality sticker, and, if coming from the UK or Ireland, headlights must be adjusted for driving on the right. Full details are available from your automobile association, or from your insurance company.

The use of seat belts in front and back seats is obligatory; fines for non-compliance are stiff. A red warning triangle must be carried in case of breakdown. Motorcycle riders must wear crash helmets. The ACI (Automobile Club d'Italia; <www.aci.it/English>) gives information on-line worth consulting before your departure.

Driving conditions. Drive on the right and overtake on the left. Give way to traffic coming from the right. Speed limits: 50km/h (30mph) in town, 90km/h (55mph) on *superstradas* (indicated with blue signs) and 130km/h (80mph) on *autostradas* (indicated with green signs). Italian *autostradas* are toll roads – you take an entry ticket and pay at the other end for the distance travelled. Be careful not to enter exclusive 'TelePass' (automatic toll meter) lanes; otherwise you will be instructed to change lanes and incur a fine.

Rules and Regulations. Italian traffic police *(polizia stradale)* are authorised to impose on-the-spot fines for speeding and traffic offences such as driving while intoxicated or stopping in a no-stopping zone.

Curva pericolosa	Dangerous bend/curve
Deviazione	Detour
Divieto di sorpasso	No overtaking
Divieto di sosta	No stopping
Lavori in corso	Road works/Men working
Pericolo	Danger
Rallentare	Slow down
Senso vietato/unico	No entry/One-way street
Vietato l'ingresso	No entry
Zona pedonale	Pedestrian zone
ztl	Limited traffic zone
driving licence	**patente**
car registration papers	**libretto di circolazione**
Green Card	**carta verde**
Can I park here?	**Posso parcheggiare qui?**
Are we on the right road for ...?	**Siamo sulla strada giusta per ...?**
Fill the tank please.	**Per favore, faccia il pieno de ...**
super/normal	**super/normale**
lead-free/diesel	**senza piombo/gasolio**
I've had a breakdown.	**Ho avuto un guasto.**
There's been an accident.	**C'è stato un incidente.**

Fuel *(benzina).* Petrol (gasoline) is sold at three grades. The grades available are Super (98–100 octane), Normal (86–88 octane) and Senza Piombo (unleaded). Petrol stations are generally open 7am–12.30pm and 3–7.30pm. Many are self-service assessible by an automatic payment machine that accepts credit cards and Italian currency. Most service stations along the *autostradas* are attended 24 hours a day. Be aware that a station marked 'Gas' indicates that it has methane gas and may not offer unleaded petrol in addition.

Parking *(posteggio/parcheggio)* in Milan is highly restricted. In areas open to non-residents, a pre-paid *Sostamilano* Card, available from authorised retailers and uniformed ATM *(Azienda Transporti Municipali)* personnel, must be displayed on the dashboard or rearview mirror. The ATM operates free parking outside the city; tel: toll-free in Italy, 800-016857.

If You Need Help. Should you be involved in a road accident, contact the Carabinieri. About every 2km (1 mile) on the *autostrada* there's an emergency call box marked SOS. If you require a tow truck, call 116 for assistance, but be aware that you will be charged; be sure that you have breakdown insurance coverage before you leave home. If your car has been towed, contact the *Comando Centrale Polizia Municipale*, Piazza Beccaria, tel: 02-77271. If your car has been stolen or broken into contact the local Urban Police Headquarters *(Questura)* and get a copy of their report for your insurance claim.

E

ELECTRICITY

220V/50Hz AC is standard. An adapter *(una presa complementare)* for continental-style sockets will be needed; American 110V appliances also require a transformer *(un trasformatore).*

EMBASSIES AND CONSULATES *(ambasciata; consulato)*

Embassies are located in Rome, but each country has a Consulate office in Milan. Most of these offices are only open 9am–12pm.

Australia: Via Borgogna 2; tel: 02-7772941; fax: 02-77704242; <www.australian-embassy.it/>.
Canada: Via Vittor Pisani 19; tel: 02-67581; <www.canada.it>.
New Zealand: Via G. D'Arezzo 6; tel: 02-48012544; fax: 02-48012577; e-mail: <nzemb.rom@flashnet.it>.
Republic of Ireland: Piazza S. Pietro in Gessate; tel: 02-55187569; fax: 02-55187570.
UK: Via San Paolo 7; tel: 02-723001; fax: 02-86465081; <www.britishembassy.gov.uk>.
US: Via Principe Amedeo 2/10; tel: 02-290351; fax: 02-29001165; <www.usis.it>.

EMERGENCIES

The following telephone numbers are in operation 24 hours a day. If you don't speak Italian, it's best to find a local resident to help you, or speak to the English-speaking operator on the telephone-assisted service (tel: 170).

Police	112
General Emergency	113
Fire	115
Paramedics	118

Please can you place an emergency call to the...?	**Per favore, può fare una telefonata d'emergenza...?**
police	**alla polizia**
fire brigade	**ai vigili del fuoco**
hospital	**all'ospedale**

G

GAY AND LESBIAN TRAVELLERS

Milan is arguably Italy's most gay-friendly city, with an interesting international community of men and women working in fields of fashion, design and publishing. ARCI-gay, the national gay rights organisation, is a great source for finding gay-friendly venues. Contact ARCIGAY-Milano; Via Evangelista Torricelli 19, 20136 Milano; tel: 02-58100399; helpline 02-89401749; fax: 02-8394604.

GETTING THERE

By Air
Scheduled flights. Most transatlantic flights direct to Milan come into Malpensa, with European and domestic flights arriving at Linate *(see page 108)*. If you are considering going elsewhere in Italy, ask if you can fly into Milan and then out of, say, Rome.

Package tours can be booked or created with local travel agents or at the Compagnia Italian Turismo *(see below, under By Rail)*, Italy's national travel agency and tour operator.

By Road *(see also page 113)*.
The road system within Italy is very manageable from north to south (including ferry transport connections to Sicily and Sardinia) and accessible when arriving from France, Switzerland and Austria.

By Rail
Ferrovie dello Stato (FS), Italian State Railways (tel: 051-257911 or (848) 888088, toll-free in Italy; <www.fs-on-line.com>), will help tourists travelling by rail to plan an itinerary. Ask about discounts for students, families and senior citizens. If you plan on travelling to other cities as well, ask about Euro-Rail and Kilometric tickets.

GUIDES AND TOURS

Many of Milan's and the lake area's larger hotels can make arrangements for multilingual guides or interpreters to accompany groups as well as individuals. A tour-guide service for Milan operates from the city's main tourist office *(see page 128)*. A three-hour bus tour of Milan with Agenzia Autostradale, tel: 02-801161 departs from the Duomo, alongside the APT centre (Tues–Sun at 9.30am; around €35). On Mondays, a walking tour of the city centre is offered from the same departure point (10am; approx. €15).

Can you recommend a sightseeing tour/an excursion?	**Può consigliare un giro turistico/una gita?**
We'd like an English-speaking guide.	**Desideriamo una guida che parla inglese.**

H

HEALTH AND MEDICAL CARE

EU citizens are entitled to free emergency hospital treatment if they have form E111 (obtainable from a post office before leaving home). Keep receipts so that you can claim a refund when you return home. Bring along an adequate supply of any prescribed medication and a copy of prescriptions.

If you need medical care, ask your hotel receptionist or local consulate or Embassy to find a doctor (or dentist) who speaks English. Milan's *Servizio di Pronto Soccorso* (Accident and Emergency) functions day and night at the Policlinico hospital, Via Francesco Sforza 35 (Metro: Crocetta); tel: 02-55031.

I need a doctor.	**Ho bisogno di un medico.**
It hurts here.	**Ho un dolore qui.**

In an emergency, telephone 118 to call for an ambulance.

Pharmacies. *Farmacias* open during shopping hours *(see page 121)*. An all-night service is also available at Stazione Centrale; tel: 02-6690935.

L

LANGUAGE

Staff in the major hotels and shops in Milan and the resorts usually speak some English. Most Italians appreciate foreigners trying to communicate in their language.

M

MEDIA

Newspapers and magazines *(giornale; riviste)*. You'll be able to find English-language newspapers at airports and in city-centre newsstands *(edicole)*. For listings that are fairly straightforward even for non-Italian speakers to understand, try: *Viva Milano,* a special insert published in Wednesday's edition of Milan's daily *Corriere della Sera,* or *Tutto Milano,* a special insert in the Rome-based *La Repubblica* on Thursdays. This sports-mad country also has a daily paper, *La Gazetta dello Sport*, devoted to events not only in Italy but all over the world.

Radio and TV *(radio, televisione)*. The Italian state TV network, the RAI (Radio Televisione Italiana), broadcasts three TV channels, which compete with six independent channels. Most of the better hotels and rental properties have cable connections which show CNN Europe and CNBC all day, offering world news broadcast in English. The airwaves are crammed with radio stations, most of them broadcasting popular music. The BBC World Service can be picked up on 1209.5KHz AM in the morning and 733KHz AM in the evenings.

MONEY MATTERS

Currency *(soldi)*. Italy's monetary unit is the *euro* (abbreviated to €), which is divided into 100 *cents*. Banknotes are available in denominations of 500, 200, 100, 50, 20, 10 and 5 euros. There are coins for 2 and 1 euros, and for 50, 20, 10, 5, 2 and 1 cents.

Banks and currency exchange. Money can be changed at exchange offices *(ufficio di cambio)* in main railway stations, airports and the city centre. However, the exchange rate at these offices tends to be less advantageous than that offered by banks. The same applies to foreign currency or travellers cheques changed in hotels, shops or restaurants. Taking cash advances from ATMs *(bank-o-mat)* on your debit or credit card usually offers the best exchange rate.

Credit cards, debit cards and travellers cheques. Most hotels, many shops, service stations and restaurants honour major international credit cards. Travellers cheques are widely accepted in most cities and tourist resorts. Outside main towns, it's best to always have some cash handy. Remember to take your passport or national identity card when you go to cash a cheque.

I want to change some pounds / dollars/travellers cheques.	**Voglio cambiare delle sterline/ dei dollari/traveller cheque.**
Can I pay by credit card?	**Posso pagare con la carta di credito?**

O

OPENING HOURS *(orari di apertura)*

Banks generally open 8am–1.30pm and 2.30–4pm, Mon–Fri. Currency exchange offices at airports and major railway stations open till late in the evening, at weekends and sometimes at lunchtime.

Churches generally close for sightseeing at lunchtime, approximately noon to 3pm or even later, and discourage tourist visits during Sunday morning services.

Museums and art galleries are usually open from 9 or 9.30am to 2, 3 or 4pm, and in some cases from 5–8pm, Tues–Sat, and until 1pm on Sun. Closing day is generally Monday.

Post offices normally open Mon–Fri 8.05 or 8.30am–2 or 2.30pm; until noon on Saturday.

Shops in Milan are closed for a half-day on Monday morning; food shops usually shut for a half-day on Monday afternoon. All shops open Tues–Sat 9am–noon and 3.30–7.30pm, and some of the larger ones also open on Sundays. Shops in tourist resorts may even stay open all day, every day, in high season. Note that many shops close in August for their main annual holiday.

P

POLICE

The municipal police *(vigili urbani)* direct traffic and handle routine tasks, sometimes acting as unoffical interpreters. The *Carabinieri*, a paramilitary force, deal with violent or serious crimes and demonstrations. Their headquarters, the *Questura*, deal with visas and other complaints, and is a good point of reference if you need help from the authorities. Outside town, the Polizia Stradale patrol the roads, issue speeding tickets, and assist with breakdowns. In an emergency, dial 112 or 113 for police assistance.

Where's the nearest police station?	**Dov è il commissariato di polizia più vicino?**

POST OFFICES *(posta or ufficio postale)*

Post offices, identified by the 'PT' sign, handle faxes, mail and money transfers. The main post office at Piazza Cordusio 1 (Metro: Cordusio) offers normal mailing facilities and services weekdays 8am–7pm.

Postage stamps, available from post offices, can also be purchased at tobacconists and at some hotels.

Letterboxes are painted red; the slot marked 'Per la Città' is for local mail, while the one labelled 'Altre Destinazioni' is for all other destinations. The blue box is for expedited international post.

Where's the nearest post office?	**Dov' è l' ufficio postale più vicino?**
A stamp for this letter/ postcard, please.	**Un francobollo per questa lettera/cartolina' per favore.**

PUBLIC HOLIDAYS *(festas)*

When a national holiday falls on a Friday or a Monday, Italians may make a *ponte* (bridge) or long weekend. Banks, government offices, shops, museums and galleries usually close on the days listed below:

January 1	*Capodanno or Primo dell'Anno*	New Year's Day
January 6	*Epifania*	Epiphany
April 25	*Festa della Liberazione*	Liberation Day
May 1	*Festa del Lavoro*	Labour Day
August 15	*Ferragosto*	Assumption Day
November 1	*Ognissanti*	All Saints' Day
December 7	*Sant'Ambrogio*	Milan's Patron, St Ambrose
December 8	*L'Immacolata Concezione*	Immaculate Conception

December 25	*Natale*	Christmas Day
December 26	*Santo Stefano*	St Stephen's Day
Movable dates:	*Pasqua*	Easter
	Lunedì di Pasqua	Easter Monday

PUBLIC TRANSPORT *(trasporto publico)*

Taxis *(tassi)*. The best way to find a taxi during busy hours is to order one by phone. Otherwise, ask for the nearest taxi rank, usually found directly in or near all major piazzas. Make sure that the meter is running. Extra charges for luggage and for trips at night, on holidays, and to airports are posted inside every cab. It is normal practice to round up the fare. Beware of non-metered, unlicensed taxis. Radio-Taxi in Milan: tel: 02-6767, 02-8383 or 02-8585.

Underground/Subway *(Metrò)*. The Metro system has four lines, including a fast rail link known as the *Passante Ferroviario*. Metro line one (M1) is red; M2 is green; M3 is yellow; and the link line, M4, is blue. A bright red 'M' sign marks the station entrances. Tickets are available at newsstands, tobacconists and Metro stations, and trains run roughly from 6am to just after midnight.

Buses/trams *(autobuses/trames)* require the same tickets as the Metro. They are valid for a comprehensive 75 minutes, so if you continue a trip from the Metro to a bus, remember to time stamp it again on board, or you will risk a stiff fine. A map of the bus and tram network is available from the tourist information office *(see page 128)*, or the ATM (Azienda Trasporti Milanesi; tel: 02-745-2015; <www.atm-mi.it>), the information office in the Duomo Metro station right under the main tourist information office.

Trains. The Italian State Railway (Ferrovie dello Stato; tel: 02-63711; <www.fs-on-line.com>) offers a service with moderate fares. The green M2 Metro line serves all of Milan's railway stations. Journey times, depend on the type of train. Always remember to punch (thus validating) all tickets before boarding the train; automatic machines are found at the foot of each platform.

Italian trains are classified according to speed. Best and fastest are the **Eurostar** (first and second class; requiring supplementary fare and seat reservations), which have their own ticketing windows at all stations. Other classifications are **Intercity** (IC; first and second class; requiring supplementary fare and seat reservations) and the **Espresso** (E; first and second class; require supplementary fare and seat reservations). The **Diretto** (D) makes a number of local stops. There are two slower local trains, the **InterRegionale** (IR; first and second class) and **Regionale** (REG; second class only). Tickets can be purchased and reservations made at a local travel agency or at the railway station (allow for time).

When's the next bus/ train to …?	**Quando parte il prossimo autobus/treno per…?**
single (one-way)	**andata**
return (round-trip)	**andata e ritorno**
first/second class	**prima/seconda classe**
What's the fare to …?	**Qual è la tariffa per…?**

Ferries/Lake Cruises. A range of rapid hydrofoils and more leisurely ferries serve the lakes. Tickets can be purchased at any stop in the area. During the warm season, there are open ticket options that allow you to either travel between two points an unlimited number of times, or which allow you to get on and off at any stop; both for a determined time period.

Milan. Information and timetables only for travel on the lakes can be found at: Navigazione Lago Maggiore, Garda e di Como, Via

Lodovico Ariosto 21 (Metro: Conciliazione); tel: 02-4676101; fax: 02-46761059; <www.navigazionelagi.it>.

Lake Como. For timetables about lake cruises contact Navigazione Lago di Como, Via per Cernobbio 18; tel: 031-579211; fax: 031-570080. The main towns served by boat and hydrofoil are Como, Tremezzo, Bellagio, Menaggio, Varenna and Bellano. A car ferry links Bellagio, Cadenabbia, Varenna and Menaggio.

Lake Garda. Cruise from Desenzano all the way north to Riva del Garda in just over four hours. Contact Navigazione Lago di Garda, Piazza Matteotti 2, Desenzano sul Garda; tel: 030-9149511; fax: 030-9149520.

Lake Maggiore. Cruise anywhere between Arona at the southern end of Lake Maggiore and over the Swiss border all the way to Locarno. Stops include Stresa, Baveno, Pallanza, Intra and Laveno and the lake's three islands. For details in advance, contact Navigazione Lago Maggiore, Viale F Baracca 1, Arona; tel: 0322-233200; fax: 0322-249530.

R

RELIGION

Christianity. Italy is a Roman Catholic country, and mass is celebrated daily (several times on Sunday). On Sundays, services in English are held at S. Maria del Carmine at 10am and 4.30pm; Piazza del Carmine; tel: 02-86463365. Information about Protestant services may be obtained from Cristiana Protestante (Luterana e Svizzera), at Via M. de Marchi 9; tel: 02-6552858.

What time is mass?	**A che ora è la messa?**

Judaism. The Jewish Sabbath and other Jewish holy days are celebrated in the dually Sephardic and Ashkenazi Synagogue on Via Guastalla in the Duomo area; tel: 02-5512029.

Islam. For Muslims, there is the Moschea Al-Rahmàn; Via Cassanese 3–5, Segrate; tel: 02-26921533.

T

TELEPHONES *(telefonos)*

You can make local and international calls from the orange public telephones. In SIP (Societá Italiana per l'Esercizio Telefonico) offices (open 7am–10pm), you can also make long-distance and international calls. Some payphones accept coins and phone-cards *(scheda telefonica)*, while others accept phone-cards only; cards of various amounts can be bought from tobacconists.

To make an international call, dial 00, followed by the country code *(see below)*, then the area code (often minus the initial zero), and finally the number you are trying to reach. Remember that in Italy you must always use the city prefix even when calling within the city and between Italian cities as well. So, for Milan, dial the code 02 even when calling from within the city.

Country Codes

Australia +61	UK +44
Ireland +353	US & Canada +1
New Zealand +64	South Africa +27

Operator-assisted/collect calls within Italy	1795
International operator-assisted/collect calls	170
Directory Enquiries	12
International Directory Enquiries	176

TIME ZONES

Italy follows Central European Time (GMT + 1). From the last Sun in March to the last Sun in October, clocks are put ahead one hour.

The following box shows times across the globe when it is mid-day in Milan.

Vancouver	NewYork	London	**Milan**	Jo'burg	Sydney
3 am	6 am	11 am	**noon**	1 pm	8 pm

TIPPING

A service charge of around 15 percent is added to hotel and restaurant bills. If prices are quoted as all-inclusive, *tutto compreso*, the service charge is included, but not necessarily the IVA (VAT of 20 percent); ask if you're not sure. In restaurants, in addition to the service charge, it is customary to give the waiter a few coins extra. Bellboys, doormen, bartenders and service-station attendants all expect a tip.

Thank you, this is for you.	**Grazie, questo è per Lei.**
Keep the change.	**Tenga il resto.**

TOILETS

Toilets may be marked with a symbol of a man or a woman or the initials WC (water closet) or: Uomini (men), Donne (women). Equally, Signori with an *i* is for men, Signore with an *e* is for women.

It may cost to use toilets in train and Metro stations, so have change at hand. The toilets in bars or cafés are usually reserved for customer use only.

Where are the toilets, please?	**Dove sono i gabinetti, per favore?**

TOURIST INFORMATION OFFICES

The Italian National Tourist Office (ENIT, Ente Nazionale Italiano per il Turismo; central office: Via Marghera 2–6, 00185 Roma; tel: 06-49711; fax: 06-4463379 or 06-4469907; <www.enit.it/>; e-mail: <sedecentrale.enit@interbusiness.it) publishes detailed brochures with relatively up-to-date information on Milan, Lombardy and the lakes. They cover transport and accommodation (including campsites, *see page 109*).

The Italian National Tourist Office can be found abroad in the following locations:

Australia and New Zealand
44 Market Street, NSW 2000, Sydney; tel: 61-292-621666; fax: 61-292-621677; e-mail: <enitour@ihug.com.au>.

Canada
17 Bloor Street East Suite 907, South Tower, M4W3R8 Toronto (Ontario); tel: 1-4169254882/9253725; fax: 1-4169254799; <www.italiantourism.com>; e-mail: <enit.canada@on.aibn.com>

Republic of Ireland
47 Merrion Square, Dublin 2; tel: 01-766 397.

UK
1 Princes Street, London W1R 8AY; tel: 020-7355 1557/020 7355 1439; fax: 020-7493 6695; e-mail: <enitlond@globalnet.co.uk>; <www.enit.it>.

US
500 North Michigan Avenue, Suite 401, Chicago, IL 60611; tel: 312-64409906; fax: 312-6443019; e-mail: <enitch@italiantourism.com>; <www.enit.it>.

In Italy
Locally, you will find municipal or regional offices (APT, Azienda di Promozione Turistica) in Milan and all the major resort towns. These can be helpful with information (but not reservations) for last-minute accommodation needs.

Milan: Via Marconi 1, 20123 Milan (Metro: Duomo); tel: 02-72524301, fax: 02-72524350; Stazione Centrale: Galleria di Testa; tel/fax: 02-72524360/70.

Bergamo: Via Vittorio Emanuele 20; 24121 Bergamo; tel: 035-213185; fax: 035-230184.

Como: Piazza Cavour 17; tel: 031-269712; fax: 031-240111; <www.lakecomo.com>.

Monza: Piazza Carducci; tel/fax: 039-323222 <www.monza.net>.

Stresa: Via Canonica 8; tel: 0323-30150, fax: 0323-32561. <www.laggiomagiorre.it>

W

WEIGHTS AND MEASURES

Italy uses the metric system.

Y

YOUTH HOSTELS

There are several youth hostels *(ostello della gioventù)* The main one is west of the city centre, near the San Siro racecourse; **aig Ostello Rotta**, Via Salmoiraghi 1, 20100 MI; tel/fax: 02-39267095. (Take number 1 Metro red line to QT8.) It is open to holders of membership cards issued by the International Youth Hostels Federation. Book well in advance.

La Cordata (Casa Scout) is a privately-run hostel on Via Burigozzo, 11, 20100 MI; tel: 02-58314675. (Take the number 3 Metro yellow line to Missori.)

Cards and information are available from your national youth hostels association and from the Associazione Italiana Alberghi per la Gioventù (AIG), the Italian Youth Hostels Association, at: Via Cavour 44, 00184 Rome; tel: 06-4871152; fax: 06-4880492; e-mail: <aig@uni.net>; <www.hostles-aig.org>.

Recommended Hotels

The Italian government rates hotels from one star to 'five star L' (luxury). These ratings are based solely on amenities provided – not on appearances or quality of service. Prices almost always include some type of breakfast, but double-check when booking. Below you will find a range of lodgings throughout Milan and the lake district; always book ahead and have your faxed confirmation in hand when checking in. According to Italian law you will need to leave your passport at the desk when registering, but it will be returned to you later. Rates vary widely depending on the season and if there is a trade fair taking place; Milan's city hotels are always priced higher than the surrounding areas. All listed hotels accept major credit cards, and are wheelchair accessible unless otherwise indicated. Hotels in the lake area stay open year round, unless noted otherwise.

The price ranges below indicate a double occupancy room with bath or shower, including service and IVA (sales taxes) in high season. These prices should be used as guides only.

€€€€	250 euros and above
€€€	150–250 euros
€€	75–150 euros
€	below 75 euros

MILAN

Antica Locanda Leonardo €€ *Corso Magenta 78; tel: 02-463317; fax: 02-48019012; <www.leoloc.com>.* Set back in a quiet courtyard down the street from Leonardo da Vinci's *The Last Supper*, this renovated hotel is tastefully decorated and welcomes guests as if they were family. Closed Christmas and three weeks in Aug. 20 rooms.

Antica Locanda dei Mercanti €€€ *Via San Tomaso 6, tel: 02-8054080, fax: 02-8054090; <www.locanda.it>.* A small but gorgeous hotel set in an 18th-century palace near La Scala. Each room is individually decorated, but common features include personal 'libraries', wrought-iron bedsteads, unusual rugs, fresh flowers and marble bathrooms. Breakfast is served in your room. A real gem.

Antica Locanda Solferino €€ *Via Castelfidardo 2, tel: 02-6570129, fax: 02-6571361; <www.anticalocandasolferino.it>*. In a great location in the lively Brera district is the Antica Locanda Solferino, a lovely old-fashioned, romantic hotel. The rooms are furnished with antiques, and most have good-sized bathrooms; breakfast is served on beautifully presented trays in your room. The owners are friendly and speak good English. The hotel is very popular, so book well in advance. The Ristorante Solferino next door is highly recommended.

Ariston €€ *Largo Carrobbio 2, tel: 02-72000556, fax: 02-72000914; <www.brerahotels.com/ariston>*. The Ariston is a so-called 'ecological' hotel, managing to be both environmentally correct and comfortable. Rooms are well furnished, and the atmosphere is friendly. All guests have unlimited use of the hotel bicycles. Handy for the canal district.

Aspromonte € *Piazza Aspromonte 12–14, tel: 02-2361119, fax: 02-2367621; <www.venere.it/milano/aspromonte>*. Small, basic budget hotel that stands out from its competitors owing to its pretty garden, where breakfast is served in summer. All rooms have TV, air conditioning and their own bathroom facilities.

Carrobbio €€€€ *Via Medici 3; tel: 02-89010740; fax: 02-8053334; <www.hotelcarrobio.it>*. A short distance from the Duomo in a shopping area close to cafés and an up-and-coming arty neighbourhood. Traditional décor. Attractive terrace. 56 rooms.

Four Seasons €€€€ *Via Gesù 8; tel: 02-77088, fax: 02-77085000; <www.fourseasons.com>*. The Four Seasons is universally acknowledged as Milan's best hotel, both in terms of atmosphere and pure, unadulterated luxury. Converted from a 15th-century monastery, with lovely rooms overlooking delightful cloisters, it is favoured by celebrities and the fashion pack. It is also home to the magnificent Il Teatro gourmet restaurant. 118 rooms.

Grand Hotel Brun €€€ *Via Caldera 21; tel: 02-45271, fax: 02-48204746; email: <brunrest@tin.it>.* Tranquil location out of the bustle of the centre; convenient for any trade fair (and the football stadium). Private parking available. 324 rooms.

Grand Hotel Duomo €€€€ *Via San Raffaele 1; tel: 02-8833, fax: 02-86462027; <www.grandhotelduomo.com>.* Built in 1860 and recently redesigned, this hotel is in an excellent location overlooking the Duomo – it's even built in the same marble. Some rooms have film themes. Lovely roof terrace. 158 rooms.

London €€ *Via Rovello 3; tel: 02-72020166, fax: 02-8057037.* Simple, clean and centrally located near the Castello Sforzesco. Air-conditioned in the summer and well heated in the winter. Specify whether you need a room with or without a shower when you book. Great budget hotel. Closed Aug and Christmas. 33 rooms.

Manin €€€–€€€€ *Via Manin 7; tel: 02-6596511; fax: 02-6552160; <www.hotelmanin.com>.* Friendly, standard hotel in the Golden Tulip chain but managed by the family who have been in charge since 1904. Attractive situation overlooking the Giardini Pubblicci. All mod cons. Closed 3 weeks in Aug. 118 rooms.

Meridien Excelsior Gallia €€€€ *Piazza Duca d'Aosta 9; tel: 02-67851; fax: 02-66713239; <www.excelsiorgallia.it>.* Situated next to the main station, this recently renovated grand institution offers all the commodities a client could desire. Lush décor with a lot of gold trim and red velvet. Fabulous breakfasts. 250 rooms.

Palace €€€€ *Piazza della Repubblica 20; tel: 02-63361; fax: 02-654485; <www.westin.com>.* A prime example of imperial Napoleonic luxury in décor and service. One of the busiest hotels with a constant flow of international expense-account patrons through their rotating doors. Closed Aug. 244 rooms.

Palazzo delle Stelline €€€ *Corso Magenta 61, tel: 02-4818431.* A lovely, atmospheric hotel with its own restaurant, all set in a former orphanage in one of the city's most upmarket districts. Attractive patio-garden.

Pensione Argentario € *Corsa Porta Vittoria 58; tel: 02-5464532; fax: 02-5464532.* This budget *pensione* is fairly central, impeccably clean and offers friendly service. At these prices, expect showers to be separate and no television. 25 rooms.

Pierre €€€ *Via Edmondo de Amicis 32; tel: 02-72000581; fax: 02-8052157; <www.hotelpierre.it>.* Ultra-modern hotel with details such as telephones in the bathroom and remote-control window shades. International clientele and friendly service, located very near the Duomo. 51 rooms.

Principe di Savoia €€€€ *Piazza della Repubblica 17; tel: 02-62301; fax: 02-6595838; <www.luxurycollection.com>.* Now combined with the Duke next door, this top-of-the-line hotel just down the street from the station offers all modern comforts amid grand, 19th-century-style décor. 399 rooms.

Sempione €€ *Via Finocchiaro Aprile 11; tel: 02-6570323; fax: 02-6575379.* A quiet, friendly establishment located north of the centre and with an on-site restaurant. Happy to accommodate small pets. 43 rooms.

BERGAMO

Miralago € *Via 4 Novembre 12; tel/fax: 035-968008; <www.hotelmiralago.com>.* Located a short distance out of town, this hotel-restaurant has a tennis court, a park and views of Lake Iseo. 45 rooms.

L'Excelsior San Marco €€ *Piazza della Republica 6; tel: 035-366111; fax: 035-223201; <www.hotelsanmarco.com>.* Modern sleek hotel with roof garden just five minutes from the centre of Bergamo. Amenities include in-room faxes and jacuzzis. 163 rooms.

PAVIA AND MONZA

De la Ville €€€€ *Viale Regina Margherita 15, Monza; tel: 039-382581; fax: 039-367647; <www.hoteldelaville.com>.* Directly in front of the Villa Reale park, this lodging with traditional décor offers a peaceful place for Grand Prix fans to relax. Restaurant plus sauna and pool. Closed Aug and Christmas. 62 rooms.

Moderno €€€ *Viale Vittorio Emanuele 41, Pavia; tel: 0382-303401; fax: 0382-25225; <www.hotelmoderno.it>.* Stylish and totally renovated hotel with slick minimalist décor close to Pavia's railway station. Bike hire is included in the room rate. Other facilities include a spa/fitness suite and bar. Closed one week in Aug and at Christmas. 54 rooms.

LAKE MAGGIORE

Grand Hotel Bristol €€€ *Corso Umberto 73, Stresa; tel: 0323-32601; fax: 0323-33622; <www.grandhotelbristol.com>.* Grand lakeside hotel, renovated in 2002, with luxurious rooms facing the gardens or the lake. For the décor, think lavish, such as crystal chandeliers and Tiffany-glass cupolas. Boasts the only indoor pool in town, and there's an outdoor pool and lakeside watersports as well. Part of the upmarket Zacchera chain. Closed mid-Nov–Feb. 270 rooms.

Grand Hôtel des Iles Borromées €€€€ *Corso Umberto 67, Stresa; tel: 0323-30431; fax: 0323-32405; <www.borromees.it>.* A grand monument among resort hotels since 1861, set in a superb lakefront parkland. Every modern comfort, tennis, golf, sauna and two swimming pools. 180 rooms.

Rigoli € *Via Piave 48, Baveno; tel: 0323-924756; fax: 0323-925156; <www.hotelrigoli.com>.* Small, peaceful hotel with a terrace garden, its own private beach and lakefront views of the Borromean Islands. Convenient location for cruises located north of Stresa. Owned by the same family since 1954. 31 rooms.

Verbano €€ *Isola Pescatori (Borromean Islands), Via Ugo Ara 2; tel: 0323-30408; fax: 0323-33129; <www.hotelverbano.it>*. Guests find peace and tranquillity on 'Fishermen's Island' and enjoy summer meals on the popular panoramic terrace of this romantic hotel. Each room is named after a flower, such as camellia, daisy and azalea, with furnishings and colour schemes to match. Delightful. Jet skis available to rent. Closed Jan–Feb. 12 rooms.

Villaminta €€€ *Via Nazionale del Sempione 123, Stresa; tel: 0323-933818; fax: 0323-933955.* North of town, offering great lakefront panoramas of the Borromean Islands and overflowing flower-garden views. Tennis, swimming pool and private beach. Closed Nov–Mar. 68 rooms.

LAKE VARESE

Motor Hotel Varese Lago €€ *Via Macci 61; tel: 0332-310022; fax: 0332-312697; <www.hotelvareselago.com>*. Motels are becoming increasingly popular in Italy, and this one is just off the main road and 4km (2½ miles) from the centre of Varese. With more character than most, it offers a pool, gym, Turkish baths and beauty centre. 44 rooms.

LAKE COMO

Grand Hôtel Villa d'Este €€€€ *Via Regina 40, Cernobbio; tel: 031-3481; fax: 031-348844; <www.villadeste.it>*. Palatial resort-hotel, one of the world's finest; 16th-century villa in flowering lakefront gardens. All amenities such as golf, tennis, squash, three swimming pools, watersports and excellent restaurants. Closed Dec–Feb. 158 rooms.

Grand Hotel Tremezzo €€€€ *Località Tremezzo, Como; tel: 0344-42491; fax: 0344-40201; <www.grandhoteltremezzo.com>*. Grand furnishings in a 19th-century-style villa overlooking Lake Como. The hotel's groomed park includes tennis, heated swimming pool and private parking. Closed Dec–Feb. 98 rooms.

Tre Re €€ *Via Boldoni 20, Como; tel: 031-265374; fax: 031-241349; <www.hoteltrere.com>.* This Como hotel is housed in a former 16th-century convent, in a quiet, convenient location near the cathedral. Bedrooms are simple but reliably clean; communal rooms are elegant. Closed at Christmas. 41 rooms.

Villa Flori €€€ *Via Cernobbio 12, Como; tel: 031/33820; fax: 031/570379; email: <lariovillaflori@galatica.it>.* Situated west of town, with lakefront gardens and mountain backdrop. 45 rooms.

LAKE GARDA

Coste € *Via Tamas 11, Limone; tel: 0365-954042; fax: 0365-954393; email: <hotelcoste@hotelcoste.com>.* Romantic hotel on the waterfront offering quaint rooms, a private pool and an olive grove behind. Parking available. Closed Nov and Dec. 30 rooms.

Grand Hotel Fasano €€€€ *Corso Zanardelli 190, Fasano, Gardone Riviera; tel: 0365-290220; fax: 0365-290221; <www.grand-hotel-fasano.it>.* An old Hapsburg hunting lodge situated in a beautiful lakeside park. Tennis, swimming pool and beach. Perfect for rest and relaxation. Closed mid-Oct–Apr. 75 rooms.

Laurin €€€€ *Viale Landi 9, Salò; tel: 0365-22022; fax: 0365-22382; email: <laurinbs@tin.it>.* Elegant, Liberty-style villa with frescoed salons and a pool surrounded by gardens. Full watersport facilities. Closed 1 Dec– 20 Feb. 38 rooms.

Villa del Sogno €€€–€€€€ *Via Zanardelli 107, Fasano, Gardone Riviera; tel: 0365-290181; fax: 0365-290230; <www.gardalake.it/villadelsogno>.* A villa turned hotel with grand lakeside gardens, tennis, sauna and pool. Closed Oct–Apr. 35 rooms.

Villa Fiordaliso €€ *Via Zanardelli 150, Gardone Riviera; tel: 0365/20158; fax: 0365/290011.* Intimate, historic and luxurious Belle Epoque villa in a gorgeous lakeside setting, with well-reputed gourmet restaurant. Closed 20 Nov–10 Feb. 7 rooms.

Recommended Restaurants

Northern Italian cuisine is identified by its butter, cream and cheeses from the mountains; rice and polenta from the plains. Look for these ingredients mixed with other regional specialities in any pizzeria, trattoria, osteria or ristorante listed below. Whenever possible, make reservations, since frequent trade shows fill up even out-of-the-way eateries. Join up with the locals for a lunch-time stop in a paninoteca for a tasty sandwich or in a casual bar for a simple bite, then enjoy a splurge on a fabulous dinner.

Closing days vary, especially in the smaller lake towns. In Milan, Sunday is the usual *giorno di riposo* or day of rest. Resort towns tend to close down in the winter and Milan during the month of August, so your selection will be limited during those periods. Eating out is generally more expensive in Milan than outside it, but you can always be price conscious and eat well at the same time by ordering wisely.

The following categories cover a three-course meal, cover and service charges, but not wine or any gratuities. Ranges are given as guides only.

€€€€	above 50 euros
€€€	30–50 euros
€€	15–30 euros
€	below 15 euros

CENTRAL MILAN

Al Cantinone €€ *Via Agnello 19; tel: 02-86461338; fax: 02-86462898.* Family restaurant with great antipasti, Tuscan specialities and Milanese favourites. All desserts are homemade. Major credit cards; closed Sat afternoons and Sun.

Bagutta €€€ *Via Bagutta 14; tel: 02-76002767; fax: 02-799613; <www.bagutta.it>.* Cheerful, well-known trattoria, where the first

Italian literary prize was born and is still bequeathed annually. Enjoy a savoury plate of *rigatoni alla Bagutta* or freshwater fish in the garden (weather permitting) while rubbing elbows with a famous soccer player or reclusive painter. Major credit cards; closed Sun, most of Aug and Christmas.

Bice €€€ *Via Borgospesso 12; tel: 02-76002572; fax: 02-76013356.* Menu comprised of Milanese and Tuscan specialities, from white truffle dishes in season to homemade pasta. This longtime popular spot for the fashion world spawned several Bice siblings in a number of international cities. Major credit cards; closed Mon, Aug and 24 Dec–6 Jan.

Panino Giusto € *Piazza Beccaria 4, tel: 02-76005015.* One of four locations in Milan displaying the crest of the Earl of Sandwich at the entrance, assuring the quality of their tasty *panini* (sandwiches). Vegetarians will have no problem here and desserts promise a filling yet inexpensive meal. No credit cards; open until 1am; closed Sun.

Peck €€€–€€€€ *Via Victor Hugo 4; Tel/fax: 02-876774; email: <cracco-peck@peck.it>.* Very chic spot for a quick-paced business lunch, and a fixed and à la carte dinner menu offering creative twists on classic Italian dishes. Distinguished wine cellar contains more than 1,700 international labels. Major credit cards; closed Sun and first three weeks of July.

NORTH OF THE CENTRE

Alfredo-Gran San Bernardo €€€ *Via Borgese 14; tel: 02-3319000; fax: 02-6555413.* A popular, reliable place for classic Milanese dishes. Try the *risotto milanese, cotolette alla milanese* and the *cazzoeula*, a pork and cabbage stew served over a bed of polenta. No credit cards; closed Sun, 20 Dec–20 Jan, and mid-July–Aug.

Al Girarrosto da Cesarina €€€€ *Corso Venezia, 31; tel: 02-76000481.* A classic Milanese choice known for the house speciality of *polpetone* (a single, oversized meatball) made from Mamma's recipe. Grilled meat or fish in simple Tuscan style are the entrées of choice for the top fashion models who dine here. Great desserts made in-house. Major credit cards; closed Sat and Sun at lunch, Aug, last week of Dec and first week of Jan.

Antica Trattoria della Pesa €€€ *Viale Pasubio 10; tel: 02-6555741; fax: 02-29005157.* Family trattoria serving traditional Lombard cooking. Try the *riso al salto*, a crispy pancake of rice lightly fried in butter – very Milanese and very good. Major credit cards; closed Sun.

Insalatiera delle Langhe €€ Corso Como 6; tel: 02- 6595180, fax: 02-29006859. Casual salad bar offering more than 20 light lunch, dinner or late-night options. Possibility of ordering hot dishes from their adjoining Piemontese (and more formal) dining room. Major credit cards; closed Sun.

SOUTH, WEST AND EAST OF THE CENTRE

Aimo e Nadia €€€€ *Via Montecuccoli 6; tel: 02-416886; fax: 02-48302005.* Well worth the cab ride and the splurge, this husband-and-wife team has created a legend in Milanese (and Italian) dining. Only the best seasonal local produce finds its way to their daily menu, featuring both fish and meat cooked with delicacy and finesse. An impressive local cheese selection and excellent wine list make for a unique experience. AmEx only; closed Sat lunch, Sun and Aug.

Da Giacomo €€–€€€ *Via Sottocorno 6; tel: 02-76023313.* Lovely setting for a Tuscan menu featuring seafood. Order porcini mushrooms in season, homemade pasta stuffed with various shellfish, and the grilled catch of the day. Major credit cards; closed Mon.

Pizzeria Il Mozzo € *Via Ravizzi 1 tel: 02-4984676.* Authentic Neapolitan pizza baked personally for you in a wood-burning oven. Other dishes are available, but this thick-crusted plateful will make the perfect simple meal. No credit cards; closed Wed and Aug.

NAVIGLI (CANAL DISTRICT)

El Brellin €€€ *Lavandai Alzaia Naviglio Grande 14; tel: 02-58101351; fax: 02-89402700*. Old-fashioned restaurant named after the washboards once used in the adjacent canal by housewives for laundry. Live piano on Sat and brunch on Sun. Major credit cards except AmEx; closed Sun dinner and Aug.

Posto di Conversazione €€ *Alzaia Naviglio Grande 6; tel/fax: 02-58106646*. An old-time characteristic canal-district trattoria. Seasonal specialities, with a menu that changes daily from meat to fish to vegetarian selections. A great dish for two or more is the sea-bream baked inside a loaf of bread. Major credit cards.

Scaletta €€€€ *Piazzale Stazione Genova 3; tel/fax: 02-58100290; <www.ristorantescaletta.it>*. Creative haute cuisine with both à la carte and *degustazione* menu. Focused on fish, the *tortino di polipo* featuring octopus is a favourite. Lovely alfresco garden dining in season. Major credit cards; closed Sun and two weeks in Aug.

BERGAMO

Da Vittorio €€€€ *Viale Papa Giovanni XXIII 21, Città Bassa; tel: 035-213266; fax: 035-210805*. Considered to be one of Italy's leading restaurants, serving regional specialities in grand style. Try seasonal scampi *carpaccio* with onion purée or crispy suckling pig. Major credit cards; closed Wed and Aug.

Taverna del Colleoni €€€ *Piazza Vecchia 7; tel: 035-232596; fax: 035-2331991*. Elegant dining room with vaulted ceilings in a Bramante palace. Local fare often features the market's fresh fish and homemade pasta. Exquisite desserts. Major credit cards; closed Mon.

Trattoria del Teatro €–€€ *Piazza Mascheroni 3; tel/fax: 035-238862*. This family-run trattoria serves local fare and is very proud of its *cassoncelli* (a type of ravioli) and *faggiano brassato* (braised pheasant) with polenta. No credit cards; closed Mon.

PAVIA AND MONZA

Al Cassinino €€€€ *Via Cassinino 1, Pavia; tel/fax: 0382-422097.* Stylish restaurant, off the main road from the Certosa, serving varied poultry and seafood as well as homegrown vegetables. Limited seating and always busy. No credit cards; closed Wed.

Antica Osteria del Previ €€ *Via Milazzo 65, località Borgo Ticino, Pavia; tel: 0382-26203.* A long-time favourite stopover for businessmen en route to or from Milan. Dig into a bowl of homemade soup, polenta or deer simmered in red wine. Major credit cards except AmEx; closed lunch in July, Aug and two weeks in Jan.

Derby Grill €€€ *Viale Regina Margherita 15; Monza tel: 039-382581; fax: 039-367647.* Dine surrounded by antiques and enjoy dishes that focus on meat or fish prepared in classic Lombard style. Excellent service and fine wine selection. Major credit cards; closed Sat lunch, Sun, Christmas, New Year and Aug.

LAKE VARESE

Teatro €€€ *Via Croce 3, Varese; tel: 0332-241124, fax: 0332-280994.* Elegant and conveniently located right in the old town centre, serving classic fare. For a twist on risotto, here it is served in a bowl of homemade bread. Major credit cards; closed Tues and Aug.

LAKE MAGGIORE

Da Cesare €€€ *Via Mazzini 14, Stresa; tel: 0323-31386; fax: 0323-933810; <www.dacesare.com>.* Family-run operation in the historic town centre. Diners can enjoy fresh catches from the lake, as well as more hearty lamb and rabbit dishes. Outside seating available, weather permitting. Major credit cards; closed Tues in winter.

Rigoli € *Via Piave 48, Baveno; tel: 0323-924756; fax: 0323-925156; <www.hotelrigoli.com>.* Local recipes using both freshwater fish and finds from the surrounding forest. Part of a private hotel that enjoys a peaceful location, the kitchen is also known for desserts made in-house. Major credit cards; open daily.

LAKE COMO

Al Giardino €€–€€€ *Via Montegrappa 52, Como; tel: 031-265016; fax: 031-300143*. Elegant garden villa sets the mood for an *osteria*-style meal of fresh fish from the lake. Small and friendly. Ask the staff to suggest the best dish of the day. Major credit cards; closed Mon, Jan and the second half of Aug.

Busciona € *Via Valassina, Bellagio; tel/fax: 031-964831; <www.vademecumitalia.com/labusciona>*. Friendly trattoria serving both fish and meat, with fabulous lake views. In the winter, try the warming braised wild goat served with polenta. Major credit cards; closed Mon and Oct.

Porticciolo €€€ *Via Valsecchi 5/7, Lecco; tel: 0341-498103; fax: 0341-258438*. The perfect place for romantic fireside dinners in winter and garden dining in summer. It's a mainly seafood menu, although vegetarians will be satisfied as well. Major credit cards; dinner only, closed Mon and Tues.

LAKE GARDA

Castello Malvezzi €€€ *Via Colle San Giuseppe 1, Desenzano del Garda; tel: 030-2004224; fax: 030-2004208*. Set in a 16th-century castle, this friendly restaurant serves creative freshwater fish dishes. Look for a mixed fish shish kebab or half-moon-shaped ravioli dressed with oysters and fresh tomatoes. Major credit cards; closed Mon, Tues, Jan and Aug.

Esplanade €€€–€€€€ *Via Lario 10, Desenzano del Garda; tel/fax: 030-9143361*. A highly acclaimed establishment in a quaint lakeside garden setting. Come here for unusual dishes such as eel and whitebait. The winter menus feature warming pumpkin and radicchio in various combinations. Major credit cards; closed Wed.

INDEX